Drawing
Attention

T0376118

© RIBA Publishing, 2023

Published by RIBA Publishing, 66 Portland Place, London, W1B 1AD

ISBN 978 1 91412 438 9

The right of Hamza Shaikh to be identified as the Editor of this Work has been asserted in accordance with the Copyright, Designs and Patents Act 1988 sections 77 and 78.

All rights reserved. No part of this publication may be reproduced, stored in a retrieval system, or transmitted, in any form or by any means, electronic, mechanical, photocopying, recording or otherwise, without prior permission of the copyright owner.

British Library Cataloguing-in-Publication Data
A catalogue record for this book is available from the British Library.

Commissioning Editor: Alex White
Production: Richard Blackburn
Designed and typeset by The First 47
Printed and Bound in the UK by Whitewater Print Media Ltd
Cover image: Architectural Press Archive / RIBA Collections

While every effort has been made to check the accuracy and quality of the information given in this publication, neither the Author nor the Publisher accept any responsibility for the subsequent use of this information, for any errors or omissions that it may contain, or for any misunderstandings arising from it.

All quotes from external sources in the book were made in private correspondence with the author.

All image copyright belongs to the Contributor of the corresponding chapter, with the following exceptions: pviii and p1 © Perry Kulper; pp5, 9, 13 (c) Hamza Shaikh p120 (bottom right) © Perry Kulper and Saumon Oboudiyat; p121 (top left) © Perry Kulper and Mark West; p198 (top right) © Pauline Personeni and Barri Studio; p198 (bottom right) © Pauline Personeni and Microclimat Architecture; p199 (bottom right) © Pauline Personeni and Mesura.

www.ribapublishing.com

Drawing Attention

Hamza Shaikh

RIBA Publishing

Contents

There's only one thing stronger than someone who truly believes in you and your immense potential – and that is your own self-belief. Pair that with a deep humility of knowing how little you know, and you will be an unstoppable force.

Go out quietly confident into the world … tread lightly with truth and purpose, and don't stop.

Hamza Shaikh

Acknowledgements

This book opportunity emerged in true serendipity and the RIBA Publishing team were the utmost pleasure to work with. I would like to thank firstly Helen Castle, whose vision and openness allowed me this opportunity; Alex White, whose guidance, patience and diligence brought this book to life; and all who helped this project progress so seamlessly in the RIBA team.

I want to mention Ele Paul and Zain Al-Sharaf Wahbeh, who helped me graphically format the template plan for this book in its earliest stages. This exercise motivated me to keep the vision going and their feedback gave me the confidence to pursue the idea further.

Of course, a big thanks to all the incredible contributors named in this book, who believed in the vision and worked hard to contribute while working on many other things. Their diligence and commitment have been a critical part of this project's success.

My good friend Adam Dudley-Mallick has supported my endless and absurd ideas with excellent honest critiques, which has been a massive support.

My parents instilled within me unwavering ambition and resilience – their endless support has picked me up in my most difficult times.

My deepest gratitude goes to my wife Naomi Shaikh, whose patience, support and belief keeps me upright.

Finally, I want to acknowledge all the talented illustrators, artists, entrepreneurs and outright architectural innovators, some who I know from social media, and some who I am yet to know. If I could have, I would have included hundreds of contributors in this book. Keep pushing the boundaries and let's hope this is just the beginning of an exciting future in our field.

About the Editor

Hamza Shaikh is a London-based architect and artist. He is prominently known for his experimental architectural drawings on social media as well as his thought-leadership in the design industry. He is the host of the *Two Worlds Design* podcast series which aims to uncover the hidden potential of architecture by speaking with extraordinary practitioners. In 2021, he was the recipient of the Individual of the Year award by the Thornton Education Trust for 'inspiring future generations' in architecture. Hamza has been described as a rising star and an influencer in the profession and is seen as a mentor to young professionals and students. He is also a regular visiting critic at the University for the Creative Arts and the University of Westminster.

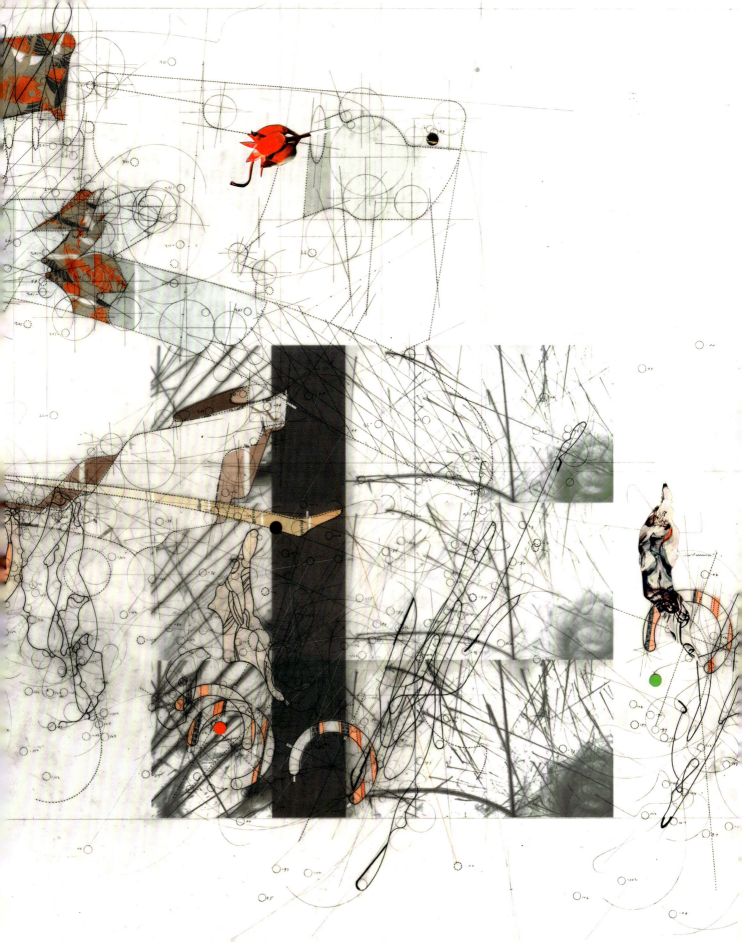

Architecture in the Age of Social Media

Hamza Shaikh

Instagram and social media have become primary resources for architectural inspiration for students and young practitioners. A collective shift towards social media as an ideas base has meant that traditional outlets, such as major magazines, are no longer the gatekeepers of success in architecture.

The propulsion of one's career is no longer quite so caught up with 'who you know'; instead, rising stars and influencers are emerging by sharing their work online. The era of starchitects may well be ending; however, the age of the 'architectural influencer' is upon us.

But what do we make of this algorithmic revolution? How fair is this algorithm, and what is the constant need for attention doing to the wider architectural discourse in education and practice?

Since my second year of university, I have been sharing my architectural drawings and ideas through Instagram and various other platforms. Why, might you ask?

In all honesty, it's because I wanted to build a following that I could leverage to start an architectural business in the future. I realised during university that architecture often struggles with a disproportionate balance between the skills required, average working hours and salary. Consider the almost decade-long process of becoming an architect, during which time the average income rarely rises above £35,000. However, something kept me passionate and inspired despite the lack of income and often intense hours of work. Perhaps it was the opportunity to be intensely curious about society, politics, philosophy and art, on a daily basis? Or maybe it was realising the power of architecture to improve people's lives and cause cultural shifts?

In hindsight, the aspect of architecture that I and perhaps most others find the greatest satisfaction in is the process of communicating and conveying ideas through artistic mediums which have the potential to come to life. This is arguably also our most valuable offering as architects. The fundamental iterative struggle that we go through as designers, balancing rational thinking with an edge of playfulness, is simultaneously the most difficult and satisfying part of our profession. At the heart of this defining dilemma is a crude skill. And although in the last few decades, technological innovation has evolved uncontrollably and transformed entire sectors, the field of architecture remains reliant on this one intuitive skill …

Drawing.

Drawing is the most important skill an architect has at their disposal. While visionary thinking and problem-solving may be the hallmarks of a successful architect, there would be no vision without a drawing. How else would you communicate your idea to a client? There is only so much that your words and your writing can convey when dealing with architectural ideas. A tissue paper sketch could say more than a paragraph, a chapter and maybe even a whole book. What's more, it only takes a few seconds to see a drawing and conceptualise it.

Throughout history, architects have been held in high esteem by the profession and society as master draughtsmen, akin to knights gilded with their mechanical pencils as solemn swords and their drawing boards as sovereign shields. It's only recently that drawings have moved beyond physical paper into digital and even virtual form. Looking ahead, the development of disruptive technology and software, such as non-fungible tokens (NFTs) and artificial intelligence art generators could also make a defining impact on our profession.

The demand for digital artists is growing, and so too is the pressure for students and young professionals to learn advanced artistic skills and software. Digitisation has not just expanded the range of jobs on offer in practice, but more widely, has propagated the notion of 'architect as artist'. Now when we consider Instagram, the most popular audio-visual social media platform in the world, powered by attention and accessible to all within milliseconds, we can perhaps understand why practices and professionals take it so seriously. Furthermore, social media's attention-fuelled algorithm has in many ways created a level playing field where people from any background can equally rise in prominence.

This digital shift and era of social media has quite rightly brought into question wider societal concerns around mental health and social value systems. But seldom do we discuss its positive effects, such as causing a communication revolution or being a catalyst to innovation and change – perhaps that's because it's obvious.

My intention is not to make any rudimentary claims as to what is good or what is bad. Rather, I hope to shine light on what I believe is a significant moment in the architectural drawing discourse. This book has been curated to include guidance, insights and tips from some of the leading and best emerging talents in the architectural drawing community – a niche that has begun to establish itself on Instagram. The aim is to gather their works and insights to concisely share how you can practically improve your drawing skills – an area often overlooked in architectural education.

Like me, the contributors selected have been sharing their explorative depictions and experimental drawing outcomes online for many years. Some of them are veterans in the field – architects turned academic artists – while others are emerging professionals, award-winning practitioners or freelance illustrators with architectural backgrounds. The selection is truly diverse and includes people from all around the world.

Every artist in this publication has a story to tell or an idea to convey, whether it's a complex harmony of linework depicting spatial mapping experiences or endless horizons of fictional pies falling from the sky. Through the unveiling of their architectural process and by offering an insight into their styles, you will learn how to draw so that you can communicate effectively.

The book does not aim to explicitly teach you drawing styles in a prescriptive manner for you to copy, but instead, to inspire you to create your visions equipped with a broad toolset, references and tips. Most of us recognise that university education often fails to teach drawing skills and techniques – and this book aims to fill that gap. It gives you the insights and guidance to help you improve your artistic capability by trying new drawing styles and processes.

You have unique skills and interests, which if allowed to flourish, will help you define and improve your design process. You have an idea in your mind that may be revolutionary, and someone somewhere needs to see it – we live in a world where attention is the most valuable currency and drawing could be your most valuable skill.

This is your guide to drawing attention.

Drawing Parallels: Architectural Drawing, Then and Now

Hamza Shaikh

It's not easy to find, let alone frame, the historical discourse on architectural drawings and how they've evolved over the years. In fact, it is not even clear what the definition of an 'architectural drawing' is. The first structures built in civilisation were most likely visualised as some sort of drawing. Therefore, identifying the beginning of architectural drawing discourse is like asking 'when did architecture begin?' – and I certainly won't be trying to answer this. However, we can fast forward to the 1970s, when architectural drawing discourse went through a significant shift due to the recession, in which unemployment became rife.[1]

During this time, known as the 'Great Inflation', established and renowned architects alike struggled to get clients and building opportunities as the construction industry experienced financial uncertainties. Architects attempted to keep their services alive by turning to what they knew best: drawing[2] – something that required no procurement and would keep their passions burning. Despite the struggles, which continued for the best part of two decades, the increasing awareness around the architect's ability to create art initiated important opportunities and a change in public perception. Independent initiative from renowned architects, support from institutions, and risks from acclaimed art collectors to curate never-before-seen works catalysed this.

There were three significant events in the 1970s which Kauffmann, in his 2018 book *Drawing on Architecture*, presents as pivotal moments for the changing perception around architectural drawings. The first was the release in 1975 of a self-curated book called *Five Architects*, which displayed the process and in-depth design works of Peter Eisenman, Michael Graves, Charles Gwathmey, John Hedjuk and Richard Meier. The book – showing photographs and textual descriptions, but more significantly drawings, of the architects' works – shot them to fame and, for the first time in contemporary discourse, opened discussions about 'architectural drawing as a visual art' and 'the architect as intellectual artist'.

The second event was an exhibition curated by the director of New York's Museum of Modern Art (MoMA), Arthur Drexler, who had also played a role in the inception of *Five Architects*. This exhibition followed three years after the release of the groundbreaking book, and exhibited over 200 drawings primarily consisting of students' works from the École des Beaux-Arts. The event was controversial for many reasons, including MoMA's decision to display works in the Beaux-Arts style, which seemed an antagonistic gesture given its deep Modernist roots. The exhibition and the symposia that followed it, questioning the fundamental influence of Modernism on education and practice, seemed to stand in opposition to the MoMA mission – but it had a massive impact.

The final event that shaped the future of architectural drawing discourse was Leo Castelli's 1977 Exhibition 'Architecture I'. Castelli was a world-renowned art collector and described by many as a 'trendsetter', so his vehement promotion of architectural drawing certainly led to a change in perception by the mere fact that it was *him* promoting it. In fact, his exhibition was the first time any architectural representations had been shown for sale in a private gallery.[3] Castelli's eagerness to convey the significance of the social and artistic value that architectural drawings represented, although met with scepticism by the wider art world, was pivotal in effecting change. At the opening of his exhibition, the works of world-famous architects were displayed, including Aldo Rossi, James Stirling and Robert Venturi.

The momentous decades that followed saw a domino effect take place in the architectural discourse against Modernist thought and, in parallel, the digital revolution also began to take hold. The 'Internet of Things' in time propelled us towards yet more uncertainties, questions, debates and psuedo-styles/movements. Architectural drawing as an art is still in question today, perhaps even more so due to the immense demand for software-proficient students. However, world-class university institutions certainly continue to propagate the nostalgic notion of the architect as intellectual artist.

Architectural drawing to capture public/client attention is a fundamental aspect of our function and is what separates us from the rest of the professionals in the built industry. It is what gains us opportunities to build – and the progenitors of the 1970s knew this. Today, we see students, emerging architects and even established practices all competing for attention in the same way, but we have very different tools at our disposal. Social media has allowed us to self-publish our work in a similar way to the self-promoting 'Five Architects' curating their own works in a highly visual format. The instinct to share our worth is not only unchanged, but also has gone into hyperdrive due to the instant sharing capabilities offered by social media technology. Platforms such as Instagram have enabled individuals and companies to communicate in a way never seen before. What might have been a rare architectural feature in a printed magazine or journal as recently as the late 20th century is now an instant shot of viral pixels to your pocket – freely available for all.

Instagram as Interface: The New Picture Plane

Recently, architecture, and to some degree architectural education, has been motivated by problem-solving and uncritical formalist approaches. Typical approaches range from digital form-finding, digitally concocted imagery, heavy contextual responses, typological extension and sensibility-driven approaches to emulation, copies and fakes. These are articulated through myriad vocabularies of late Modernism, high-tech, deconstruction, folding, field thinking and, more recently, topology, affect, contemporary processes and all things 'post'. These developments have shaped recent disciplinary discourses, particularly in architectural education. The Covid pandemic, and increased awareness of deeply seated structural racism have fuelled the flames of the shifting topographies of content and communication in architecture. A small number of critics, theorists and academic institutions have controlled these discourses and distributions – deciding what was fair game and what was out of bounds. This was largely done through various magazines, journals and other forms of printed material. The introduction and consumption of Instagram has produced an entirely different field of play.

Instagram's reach has increasingly lured audiences and influences away from paper-based dissemination in favour of the rapid movement of digits on smallish, rechargeable, shiny screens. Vision, constructed through a new kind of picture plane, is driven by an alternative rapid eye movement that results from tickling the seductively high-res screen, scrolling from image to image at breakneck speed, in sometimes distracted states of attention. Without a doubt, access to diverse content, to authors themselves (DM me) and to new curatorial practices, and the development of ecologies of design pockets within the forest of available content, has radically altered the visual arts, particularly architecture. From age and demographic-specific alignments, the democratic space of Instagram presents diverse content, links to other information ecologies, burgeoning social constructions, alternative techniques for working and new aesthetic influences, superseding age-old strategies of knowledge construction. A move has occurred from print-based mediums to speeding images – a move away from linework, and conventional architectural drawings, towards saturated, atmospheric and graphically rich, sometimes complex, composited, hybridised images. These developments show us the change in projections from orthography and the fixity of the picture plane to dynamic, processed, scripted and machine-learned visualisations.

Significantly, whether in the space of drawing, erasing and redrawing on sheets of paper, or in the keyboard commands of varied digital interfaces, the work of design still largely happens in the drawing, or its digital counterpart, the computer. Architectural drawings, visualisations and images continue to ground the dense and tangled relationship between the architect and a world. They provide literate grounds for communication from the architect to a construction team, or from the design studio to public sharing. On the other hand, through the rapid, sometimes uncontrolled and uncontrollable domain of Instagram, images have been composited, abstracted and hybridised, producing a plethora of meshed, geographically and temporally tangled sequences and combinations of images. Young, aspiring architecture students and architects feast on aesthetic prompts, techniques for production and the latest posts, summoning soft forms of knowledge-building. Then, they transfer and often incorporate that new knowledge into the space of design studio production.

The architectural drawing remains an operational compass for the work of the architect – its legacy is stable and vulnerable at the same time. Its history is established as well as waiting to be written. However, those influences, its roles in architectural education and its trajectories are undergoing serious reconsideration as the image proliferation of platforms such as Instagram infiltrates and co-opts more traditional forms of design. As Hamza says in the framing of this book, Instagram has become the primary resource for today's architects and young practitioners. A new wilderness, filled with curiosities, discoveries and unrequited speed has emerged. The new picture plane has arrived, forever transforming, and setting up the next gravities for architectural, spatial and cultural influence. Fasten your seatbelts and indulge in the ride. Alice's wonderland has just shifted into the Instagram meta-drive …

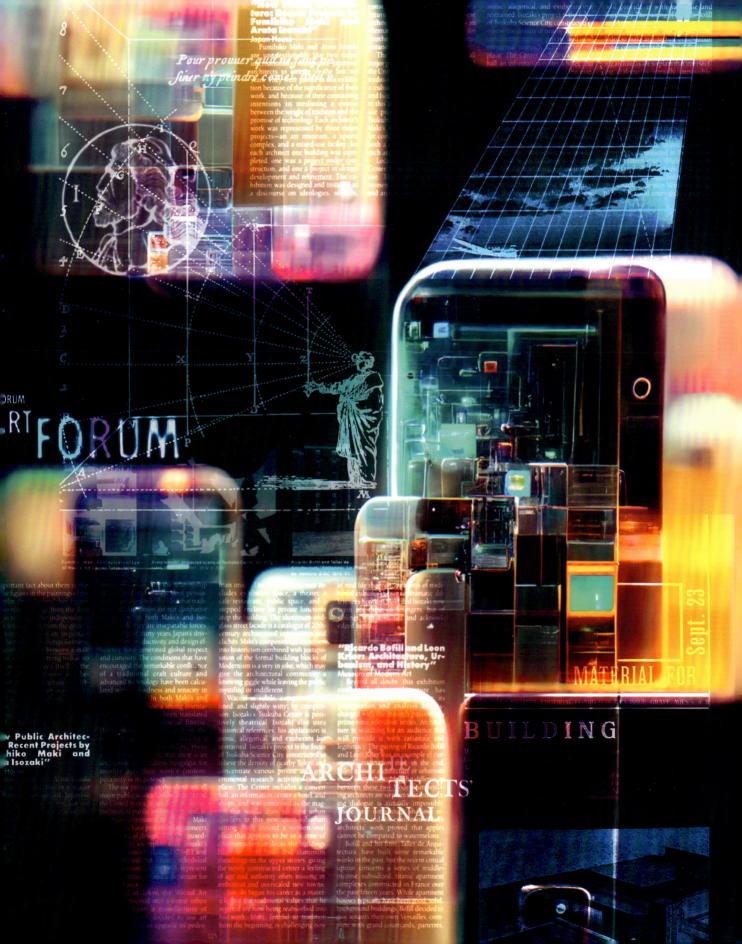

"A simple sketch could communicate the content of an entire chapter ..."

Vector Collage
Hamza Shaikh

Title:
**Architectural designer,
artist, podcaster**

Instagram:
@hamzashaikh.design

Story

I've always been obsessed with deep expression through art. During my
days in high school, I would regularly be in detention, and it was eventually
agreed by my art teachers and head of year that I could spend my detained
lunchtimes in the art studio. This was a deal negotiated out of sympathy for
my continual isolation – albeit deserved at times. However, my 'misconduct'
at school was out of sheer frustration at the monotonous routines, plain
textbooks and the numbingly uncreative environment I was in. As a result,
I began my personal artistic explorations at a young age while being
cognisant of ways to be entrepreneurial about it. Growing up, I loved
the works of Wassily Kandinsky. My mother had a print of *Yellow Red Blue*
framed in our house, and I found myself subconsciously painting in a similar
Deconstructivist, Expressionist style. Little did I know that Kandinsky's
Bauhaus-inspired works would gradually lead me into a deep interest
in architecture.

FIND ME:

Inspiration

After entering architectural education, I was enthralled by the artistic expression encouraged during the conceptual stages of a project. I was especially surprised by this, because I had always believed architecture was just about making either completely functional or ornamental buildings. I didn't know one could design using hard rationality while also being relentlessly creative. To my delight, I learned that this was the sole aim of architecture: to be rational and artistic at the same time. At this point I became passionate about learning of the world and its politics, philosophies, cultures, and sciences. I was excited to find that architecture could be used as a tool to effect positive change, drawing on multiple tangential fields in the search for harmony.

I began to love the process of trying to find big issues to solve through architecture, and I felt this is where all good concepts come from. However, after graduating and with a great deal of hindsight, I realised that all drawings start with a thought. Sometimes a simple thought – even a subconscious thought. That is why, often, my drawings are merely a record of my thoughts and instinctive ideas. I love to draw through improvisation, and some of my best drawings/designs came from just putting pen to paper and seeing what happened!

Process

I work in multiple mediums using various tools, devices and interfaces. I am obsessively curious about drawing mediums and experimenting with new forms of representation fascinates me. That is why you may find that I don't have an obvious 'style' of drawing as much as the other contributors in this book.

Committing to one style and medium of drawing is to deny myself the joy of experimenting and discovering new things. Sometimes a new drawing medium can unlock new ideas due to varying forms of expression and their differing visual effects. To name just some mediums, I use pencils, fine liners, fountain pens, marker pens, watercolours, graphite sticks, paper collages, oil pastels, **Photoshop** and iPad digital sketching tools.

Collage is my favourite way of generating compositions. I am not afraid to utilise existing drawings to generate my own ideas. I often reuse my own past drawings, finding a part of the drawing that intrigues me; I cut it out, rotate it, draw on top of it. I find textures that satisfy me; existing facades or photographs of surfaces I see around inside/outside. My methods are always changing. I don't know if I ever will commit to one style and method – I just find the experimentation too enjoyable.

Tips

Always focus on the broader
composition of drawing to start
with – details come later. It's the
same as an essay – you start with
the structure and chapters, then
you get into the details.

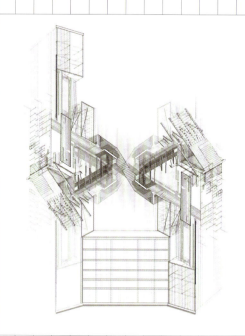

VECTOR COLLAGE

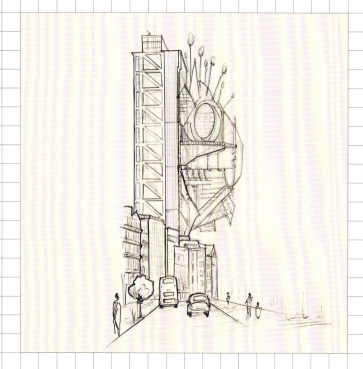

Be confident with your pencil strokes.
Hard, fast and uncontrolled movements
can make a drawing more powerful, as
it seems purposeful. Try this by doing
10-second sketches of detailed objects.

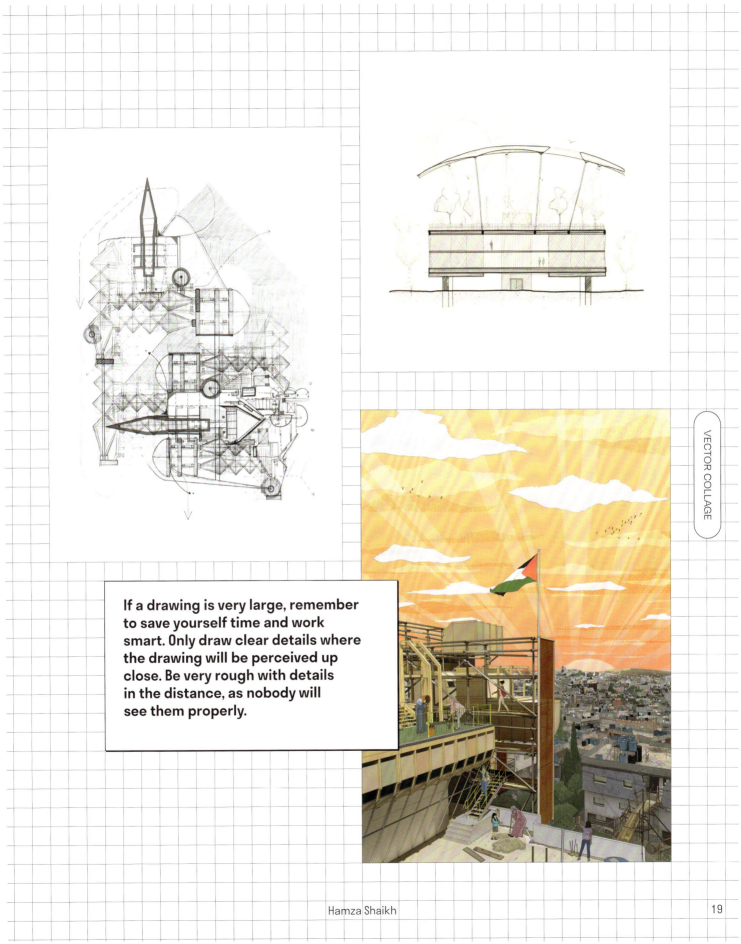

If a drawing is very large, remember to save yourself time and work smart. Only draw clear details where the drawing will be perceived up close. Be very rough with details in the distance, as nobody will see them properly.

Step by Step

You will recognise this drawing from the front cover. It is called 'Parasitic Lexicon', and I call the method of drawing 'Vector Collage'. It was initially done as an improvised sketch while I was on a train. I was experimenting with this new method of drawing where I draw extremely detailed 'pieces' and then collage them together – erasing; adding lines and textural expression where I feel they are needed. This drawing was primarily a composition exercise, but my underlying interests in parasitic architecture inspired it. It could be described as a sectional drawing denoting a parasitic spatial system embellished with an architectural lexicon. This type of drawing is instinctive to me, and for that reason, if I was ever to commit to a specific style of artistic expression, it would be this.

When I was thinking of a front cover for this book, I thought about the concept of creating a drawing which expressed the notion of 'drawing as communication'. I instantly realised that my early sketch of this drawing would be perfect, because it already used symbolism and abstracted architectural language. However, I decided to take the drawing one step further by expressing the symbolism more and even writing words within the linework – making the words and artwork intertwined in true parasitic spirit. The result was a finished piece which showed that drawings and words can be indistinguishable and interchangeable as forms of communication and language.

The aim of a vector collage is to take a rough sketch collage and translate it into a vector-based drawing, maintaining its organic feel. This could seem like an impossible task, as the linework can be immensely detailed; however, an app called **Vectornator** allowed me to hand-draw vectors on my **iPad** with ease and great speed.

Tools: Vectornator, iPad, Apple Pencil, Procreate

1.

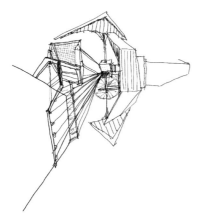

Using an **iPad**, **Apple Pencil** and the app **Procreate**, roughly draw a detailed architectural element. For me, this is a device or machine with umbrella-like arms and various tensile structures attached to it. Think about elements with architectural relevance/function. In my case, I am thinking about high-tech architecture and parasitic forms which embrace the existing built fabric. Try drawing without a reference and create your own forms, including hints of texture and materiality in the device.

2.

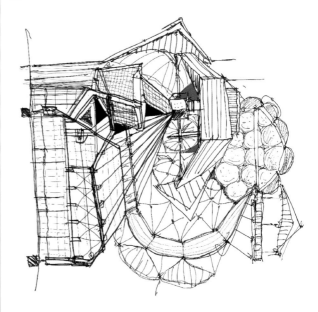

Work detail into the composition, exploring different architectural styles and forms. Fill in the gaps with texture and connective components to indicate structural realism. Introduce objects into a physical dimension, by grounding it – subjecting it to the laws of physics. Here I use an 'anchor' attaching the composition to a wall (on the left).

3.

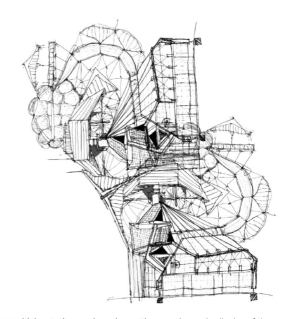

After multiple rotations and precise cutting, copying and collaging of the fragments, start to build up the composition further. By cutting different pieces out of the original fragment and its amalgamated combinations, erasing and redrawing various components, and scaling specific pieces down/up, the composition can begin to take on an architectural form.

4.

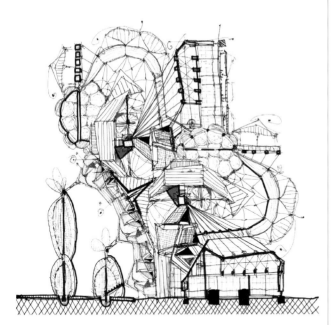

With the introduction of darker fills and thick lines to denote sectional language, the composition starts to reveal its spatial characteristics. This is where you can further introduce recognisable architectural symbolism to the drawing, such as dashed lines, crosshatches, shrubs and structure.

5.

After the digital compositional sketch collage is complete, import the JPEG into Vectornator. This app allows you to draw over the sketch with CAD/vector lines (like AutoCAD, Illustrator or MicroStation) but with the ease of a pencil stroke as opposed to the click of a mouse. This provides immense speed, control and fluidity in the vector drawing. Make sure to set up various line weights and layers properly before drawing.

6.

Within the app, using the Draw tool, draw the thickest lines that sit in the foreground of the sketch, making sure to fade this layer and create different line weights. Draw the outline of shapes that you know will need to be filled with a solid colour or texture later.

7.

You should have at least one layer of lines with a much finer weight to give the drawing real depth. These lines capture the finer details, texture/hatches and any other improvised additions.

VECTOR COLLAGE

Next, you can draw some words that seep and morph into the drawing. Draw these on a separate layer with the rest of the artwork visible so that you know how to seamlessly integrate the linework into the curves of the drawing. These don't have to be words – they could be other drawn elements.

9.

With all three of these 'families' of linework layered on top of each other, the original sketch can be represented in a crisp and detailed vector-based drawing. The composition is complete apart from the finishing touches.

10.

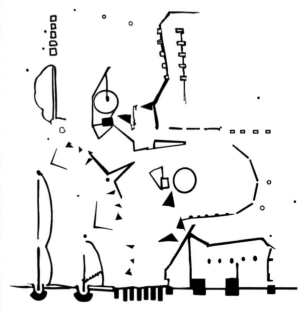

To finish the drawing, add the black solid fills in Adobe Illustrator (Vectornator is not great with solid fills). The solid black fills were a crucial part of the drawing and really show the depth of layering. By using these two different vector-based programs, you can maximise your drawing capability.

11.

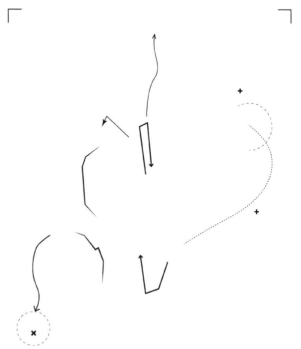

The last step is to add the embellishments – being careful not to overdo an already complicated drawing. This includes some of the architectural symbols such as arrows, hatches, radii and tonal fills.

DRAWING ATTENTION

"Don't be afraid to revisit a past drawing... New is not always better."

Machinic Assemblies
Bea Martin

Title:
Architect, educator

Instagram:
@bgommartin

Story

The 1990s were the stage for the digital shift in architectural education. During this time, I was being taught the ordered language of Modernism and classical drawing at the Lisbon School of Architecture, but I was more interested in the labyrinthine structures of Piranesi's prisons, Libeskind's Chamber Works, and the intriguing [Günther] Domenig Steinhaus drawings. It was not until I came across *Radical Reconstruction*[4] by Lebbeus Woods that drawing became a journey. Drawing has never been about the 'how'. The exciting question is 'why' and 'what does it mean?'. Working outside oneself, reading, listening, looking at things, and looking at drawings that have made a difference. Ultimately, it is not about style or technique. It is about the subject matter and the language in which we chose to materialise the response.

FIND ME:

Inspiration

In my work, a drawing is conceived as a machinic assemblage – a drawing that is multiple. Its function or meaning no longer depend on identity, but on the assemblages it forms with other drawings. My methodology draws analogies with the work of Deleuze and Guattari by exploring drawing as an assemblage: an exploration of how the drawing is put together and stratified as a subject. I argue that a drawing should, ultimately, be valued for what it can do (rather than what essentially 'is') and that assemblages should be assessed in relation to their enabling, or blocking, of a drawing's potential to become other. Concepts, or ideas, can be triggered by a flurry of different components, contextualised or acontextual. Other drawings, a certain place, some words or a particular text.

Process

It is fair to say that my work always starts structured. Co.De[Re] is a process I have been building on for a while and which I share with my students in our design studio when pushing them to 'think conceptually'. This is a three-step rationale: Construct, Deconstruct and [Re]construct. Firstly, Construct relates to an existing element – it could be a text, an urban space or an object. An analytical study ensues of said element. Secondly, Deconstruct – after the investigative study, an explorative dissection begins. Through a non-linear taxonomic approach and the ability to frame and 'edit' the fragments, a disconnect of the element from reality is propelled, and in so doing we arrive at a concept word. Thirdly, [Re]construct – this final stage is about operative speculation. Armed with a conceptual word, the testing of possibilities has a guide, not yet the solution. We are still allowing for chance accident to interfere.

That said, devising a drawing brief or defining a strategic plot, before or during the action of drawing, can be great anchor to your narrative, if it does not become formulaic. Drawing is all about being attentive, curious and intrigued. Read, see, listen, write … then draw.

Bea Martin

Tips

Revisiting a published drawing:
It is OK to revisit, amend or
change a drawing. I think of them
as machinic assemblies, where
if something is not working, you
can always modify some parts.

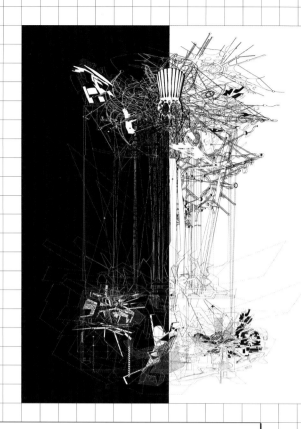

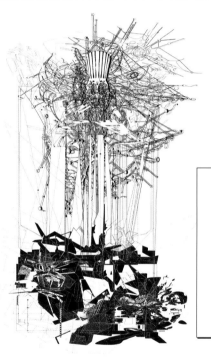

Storyboard your drawings:
Plan everything ahead! A storyboard
helps you visualise the structure of your
work and what to do – beginning, middle
and end. It gives you the opportunity and
space to think out the content and flow
of your drawing. List it, organise it, map it.

Classic references:
Do not lose sight of valuable classical
references; drawings that have stood
the test of time. For example, Étienne
Boullée's dark and pure geometry of
shadows, Auguste Choisy's rational
visualisation of buildings, or Mies van
der Rohe's restrained-yet-powerful
collages. Learn from the masters.

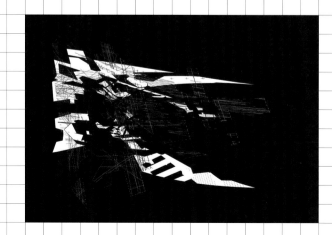

'Wow' moment:
Make sure you prioritise an element or a group of elements in your drawing – the high point of your piece. Devise a visual hierarchy from the start. There are many ways you can captivate attention. For example, you can use colour, line weight, or create several layered drawings to create depth.

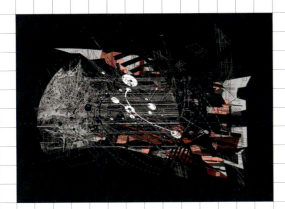

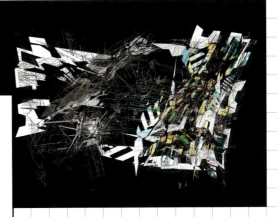

(under)inform or (over)inform:
Ask yourself, what is the information I need to get through? Think orientation, scale, dimension, print size. Be meticulous with the choice of drawing elements and clear with your message.

Step by Step

1.

The work explores *lines and traces* as a device, in order to test movement and to uncover the interrelated and intertwined nature of the site. Furthermore, it takes inspiration from the following statement:

> Perhaps … these ruptured lines are not solely broken spaces that we cannot perceive … these are the lines that simultaneously negotiate the destruction of min[e]d fields, traveling among them, leaving a trace of its origin, graphing itself and reading itself anew, opening itself always to another line, one more trace.[5]

Through conceptual and tectonic strategies, the visible lines and invisible traces become involved with and come to terms with the forces and currents of spaces yet to become. There are two distinct stages of work: the *territorialisation*, which relates to research and study of the site as a construct, and *deterritorialisation*, the breaking up of the site, which entails the deconstruction and consequential reconstruction of the conceptual element.

The Construct – a Midwestern agricultural landscape in Ames, Iowa – the exploration began with the articulation of photography, particularly through photomontage and juxtaposition of forms, aiding an understanding of the context/ site of the work.

The Deconstruct – fragmentation of the site, the different machines. Each machine is a layer of information, a codex, that is operating as a part of a folium (see previous spread). The preferred media enabled a non-linear narrative through the juxtaposition of site fragments and its ability to frame and 'edit' the field conditions, resulting in a disconnect of image from reality – the site. This phase was developed and produced solely on Rhino, with the outputs resembling a series of shop drawings.

Finally, the Reconstruct – the assemblage of all notational systems – the act of reconstructing our engagement with shrouded spaces. Each 'machine' is an individual register of field conditions. The final procedural stage is the assemblage of all these 'machines' (see bottom of previous page). Throughout, the graphic language of the drawing consists only of points, lines and hatches. A collage of lines and points rather than imagery.

In all, the varied deformation of the topographic surface enables removal from its original host space, which was later rejoined and overlapped. It no longer is a single existing continuum but rather a multilayered terrain of otherness. As such it locates and relocates the reader in relation to the site.

Tools: Rhino, Illustrator, Photoshop

1.

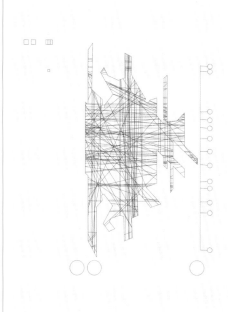

You do not have to follow a linear process – try developing pieces of compositional delineation on **Rhino** and later collaging them together. I created this first piece of drawing by mapping networks and grids of my site. Through treating the drawing as a record of data, the composition begins to emerge as a superimposed network of grids.

2.

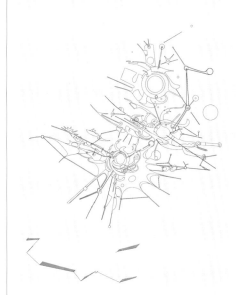

Record the key features to uncover the interrelated and intertwined nature of the site. Here I added features in a different terrain of the site while referencing connective nodes. This creates 'The [sym]biotic machine: the organic and synthetic discord' assembling elements, silos and ploughed fields.

3.

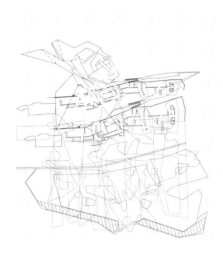

Use the plan drawings of an existing building. Erase and force thresholds together to reinterpret the structural layout in the given context. This is called 'The Intramural Machine: Interiority and the space within', redefining the boundaries of space and the formation of contiguities (vectors of movement).

4.

Create a layer to represent the spacing and intervals between matter. Try skewing your previous drawing in Step 1 to create a perspectival effect and meld lines to suit the composition. This redefines the linear armature and flow structure. The drawing details two types of contextual flows, continuous and interrupted (represented by the omission, or break, of the line).

5.

Combine compositions from the previous steps and invert the colours to reveal the inverted compositional attributes. Here, I have created the assembled shadowing stratums of light's conditioning and inner behaviour in this quick step, which becomes a vital part of the final composition.

7.

8.

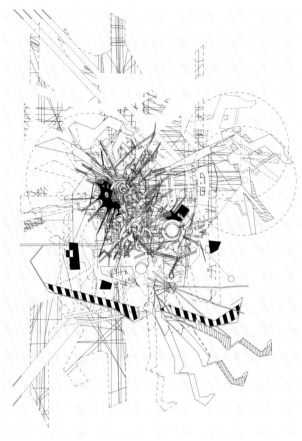

In the same way as the previous step, reuse an earlier drawing but skew, rotate and superimpose more drawing information on top of it. This drawing shows the flattening of the situated architectural devices.

Combine all the drawing pieces together in a vector collage, refining and adding embellishment wherever compositionally or conceptually needed. This is the 'Machinic Assembly'; it shows the articulation of lines as a topographic operating system rather than a category of the contextual construct; a platform rather than a site. A multilayered graphic artefact.

Bea Martin

"What if ... ?"

Drawing Attention

Creating Worlds
Eric Wong

Title:
**Architect, illustrator,
production designer,
design tutor**

Instagram:
@ericwong_folio

Story

My architectural journey has been influenced by critical thinking,
speculative architecture and intricate line drawings. I initially studied art
and architecture at the Byam Shaw School of Art, Central Saint Martins,
completing my undergraduate degree at Cardiff University and later
graduating with a Master's from the Bartlett School of Architecture, UCL

The journey from my architectural education to practising as an
architect and ongoing academic involvement has enriched the approach
I take to drawing, whether this is drawing with sensibility and naivety,
drawing with care and freedom, drawing the known and unknown, or
just learning and thinking through drawing.

FIND ME:

Inspiration

What is the narrative in the drawing I am trying to convey? Whose perspective am I seeing this view from? What other techniques can I use to show an additional level of information that I cannot in a conventional view? How can I demonstrate the intangible qualities in my proposal? Are there historical, cultural or contextual visual references I can bring in? What is the tonal atmosphere I am trying to achieve? How important is the time of day and year in the project, and how can this be visualised? These are some of the many questions I ask myself when I am composing and planning a drawing. These questions act as visual guides to help me construct a succinct and informative drawing.

The process of drawing can often be refined by building on and learning from a visual library of references. Whether it is the composition of a drawing you enjoy, the proportion of colour employed or the inventive and speculative representations of the unknown, references allow you to borrow, learn from and adapt them into your own drawings.

My advice for architectural students struggling to come up with concepts is to not be fixated on 'the big idea', but rather to enjoy the process of exploration. This can encompass developing a position in your project, creating a narrative, exploring key themes through different mediums, and learning from references that may not always be architectural. The opportunities provided by being open to exploration may help guide you towards a framework for your proposal.

Process

Drawing techniques and methods are arguably more enriching when they are informed by and inform the key themes of an architectural proposition. In Cohesion: The blueprint for a United Kingdom, the historical, cultural and contextual thinking of the proposal is situated in the British Isles; therefore, it was helpful to learn from British visual references. Inhabitation and activity are informed by the wit and characters in British illustrator Heath Robinson's inventive and humorous drawings. The mood, colour and atmospheric tones are inspired by British painter LS Lowry's depictions of romanticised British landscapes, and the architectural tectonics developed in the project borrows and learns from iconic buildings and infrastructures built in the UK.

Regarding methodology, using programs you are comfortable with can allow for confident manipulation in your visual representations, but being open to new ways of working can also create exciting and unexpected opportunities. Confidence also comes with practice, so it is helpful to continually test, experiment and refine your drawing approach.

Tips

Colours and tones can be borrowed from your key references. Here my palette was inspired by LS Lowry's paintings.

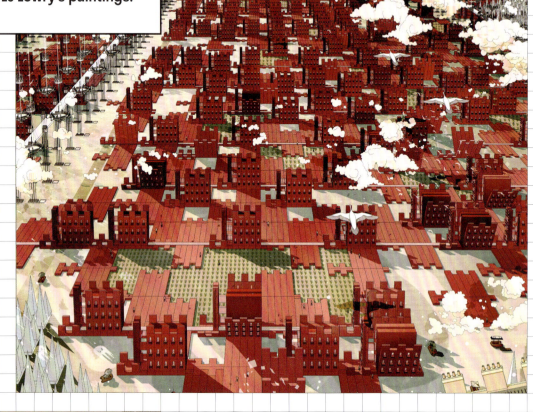

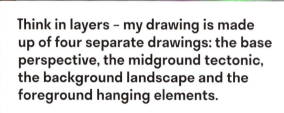

Think in layers – my drawing is made up of four separate drawings: the base perspective, the midground tectonic, the background landscape and the foreground hanging elements.

The crowns on the chandelier are inspired by the articulation of the spires in Oxford. You can use white hues to represent natural light, and yellow tones portray artificial light.

Step by Step

Each drawing starts with a sketch. An initial gut feeling composition helps to visualise the overall framework of a drawing. This is then clarified with annotations to help focus the narrative. The following drawing aims to reimagine and speculate on what happens in this New Hyde Park, but also asks: If I am to depict the activity on the ground, how can I demonstrate how the architecture is used in the view? To suggest that, the tectonic has a kitchen, smell is depicted in the drawing, puffs of smoke leave the top of the chimney, the inner lining of the cape is lined with pie icons and pies are falling out from the kitchen. The drawing aims to depict the use of both the architecture and the park. It is helpful to consider drawing as a tool to design and develop your proposal.

Tools: MicroStation 3D, MicroStation 2D, Photoshop

1.

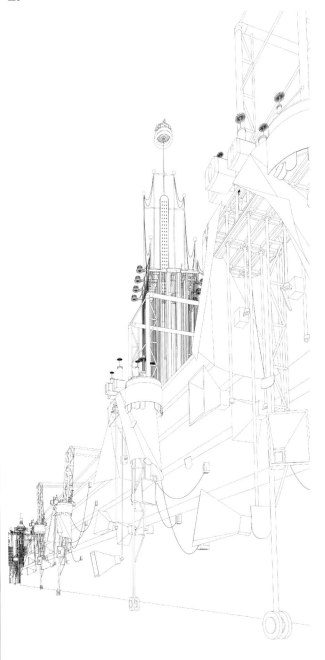

[Photoshop, MicroStation 3D]
Prepare a 3D model of your design, which can help you select key views, and adjust the base lighting and shadows. Carefully defining the position, height and angle of your light source will help you construct the contrast, depth and shadow required for your drawing.

[MicroStation 2D]
Prepare the base lines for the drawing. Certain types of drawing are better suited to either a portrait or landscape view, so it is important to consider the format of a drawing. Think about the framing and cropping of a view, as it helps to set the proportions and boundaries of the composition – whether this is amount of ground compared to sky, foreground to background or activity to architectural elements. Once the framework for the view is prepared, it can then be exported.

3.

[Photoshop]
Add base fills for the drawing. Whether inspired by key colour references related to the proposal, or whether the careful framing of the view helps to set the ratio of colour, smaller accents of colour can add variety and focus to the drawing. This sets the atmospheric and tonal ambition.

4.

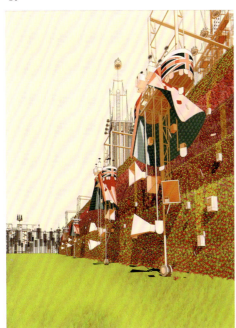

[Photoshop]
Start to add texture. Flat colours and shadows are a starting point to demonstrate the tonal quality and three-dimensionality of your drawing, but texture will start to suggest materiality, whether it is grass, fruits or fabrics.

5.

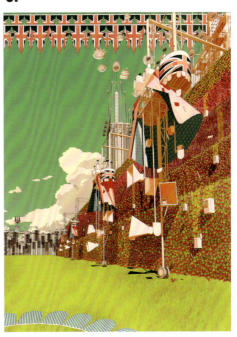

[Photoshop]
Define your background and foreground. This is suggested by the clouds and colour of the sky in the background and the bunting and picnic mats in the foreground.

6.

[Photoshop]
Composite your drawing with drawn elements that you may not have modelled. Topiary queens and hedges add a different character and layer to the drawing.

7.

[Photoshop]
Inhabitation: demonstrate how your space is used, how it comes alive and how people may occupy it. The style, choices and actions of the people you place into your drawings will start to suggest a very particular and precise use and narrative.

8.

[Adobe Photoshop]
Embellishment, activity and life: draw different types of fruits grown throughout the year, the diverse occupancy of people inhabiting the space, the various pies cooked in the city and the numerous garden activities enjoyed, through to clouds, cultural references and additional grass and topiary textures. Additional drawn moments really bring a drawing to life.

Eric Wong

Sketch Like an Architect
David Drazil

Title:
Architect, online teacher, speaker, author, founder of SketchLikeAnArchitect.com

Instagram:
@david_drazil

Communication

Sketching is about communication – about being effective in communicating your ideas. It's not about you talking and other people hearing what you say – it's about making sure that these people understand exactly what you mean. If you can sketch your idea with a pen and paper, you can convey it with any other visual medium. Knowledge and skills gained through hand sketching help you become better even as a digital artist. Observation skills, confident lines, understanding of perspective and light and shadows – all of that will help you make better architectural visualisations, conceptual diagrams, digital paintings or any other illustrations.

The sketching process

Depending on complexity, I begin either with a pencil or a pen to create a visual structure and set the right scale. Then I use pens with lighter line weights to build up the main volumes and work with different depth planes. I continue with texturing and shading, adding more of the surroundings and details. Final touches might include linework with a heavier line weight for emphasis and contrast or, optionally, use of colour.

Inspiration

As for sources of inspiration, I believe that architects shouldn't get inspired by another work of architecture – that's very limiting. Don't get me wrong, it's important to do research and mood boards with reference pictures, but that's not inspiration in the true sense. Regarding this, there is one quote from architect Edmund Bacon that really resonates with me. He said: 'It's in the doing that the idea comes.' It really does work like that for me – I get ideas during the process, very often as I sketch, because there are no barriers as with using software on a

FIND ME:

computer. The connection between your mind and your hand is very natural and it supports all the creative flows.

No rulers please
I prefer not to use rulers, because freehand sketching brings so much more freedom to both the sketching process and the dialogue that evolves from it. I perceive sketching as a means of communication more than anything else. And freehand sketching with wavy, imperfect lines leaves a lot of space for opening a creative dialogue – either between colleagues, or an architect and a client. The imperfections suggest that nothing is set in stone and that everybody is welcome to contribute with their own inputs.

Workflow
When I was a student in architecture school, I heard from my professors all the time that students didn't sketch anymore. Instead of sketching out solutions or drawing different options for elevations, students just rather jumped right into their BIM software to place default windows into generic walls and were done with the facade. Such process, where you dive into software without being clear on what you want to achieve, hurts both you as a designer and the design itself.

One tip above all

If I had to choose just one thing that is often neglected but has a dramatic impact on your sketches – it's your observation skills. Learn to observe and understand why things work and look like they do. Observation skills are essential for good sketching, for composition, light and shadows, proportions, materiality, and everything else. Train yourself to be better at observing positive and negative spaces of objects, their proportions, and spatial relations between them. It's a skill like any other, and with a little bit of practice you'll get better – and, more importantly, your sketches will improve. What I love about sketching is that it forces you to understand the object first before you're able to draw it. In that way, when you sketch you'll always learn something new.

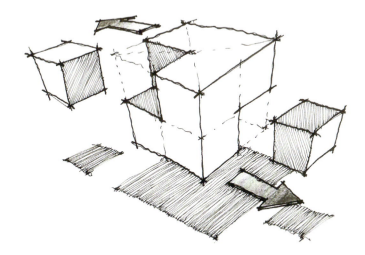

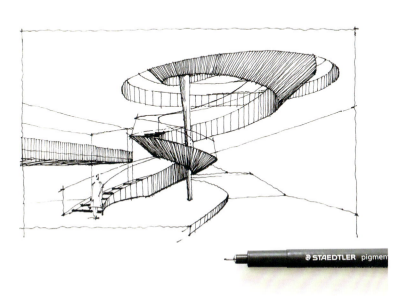

"Practice makes perfect."

Street Illustrations
Yvette Earl

Title:
**Freelance illustrator and
full-time graphic designer
at HLM Architects**

Instagram:
@yvetteearlillustration

Story

You can't force an illustration style; it must come naturally. I used to struggle working digitally as it felt like cheating, and I wanted to do everything by hand in pen ... I was very wrong! Taking pen drawings into Photoshop was a big style leap, where I discovered colour, textures and being playful with creations. I bought an iPad in 2018, downloaded Procreate and my work started to develop fast. Having a portable device allows me to draw on the go, and quickly. Alongside the digital progression, looking to other artists and styles helped me out early on. Psychedelic art inspired my colour palette and pushed me to be bold. You can see my love for LS Lowry coming through in my work, and I take inspiration from his busy city scenes full of characters and life.

FIND ME:

Inspiration

Towns and cities are a key source of inspiration. I can spot a visually appealing building or street and envision how it will look drawn in my style. Lots of ideas arrive when I'm walking or at night in bed, which is where I keep a sketchbook with ideas and rough concept sketches. We all have bad days, though, where we struggle to draw, colours aren't working and nothing is going our way, which is when I visit Pinterest for inspiration. Another source comes through soaking up the surroundings. The colour palettes in everyday life are inspiring, and keeping off your phone allows you to look up at the stunning architecture around us.

Process

I have a relatively set method for work, mainly in **Procreate**. Once I've spotted a scene I want to draw, I take lots of photos, but only during the day. I choose my light direction and how the shadows will work to give it a surreal look. I have a detailed, graphic and controlled drawing style; working with the Apple Pencil in **Procreate** works best for my approach to drawing. Be creative and find what works best for you; there is no right or wrong answer, and by experimenting you'll discover your personal style and working methods.

Tips

Often, I don't like my illustrations until they're finished. I nearly always hate how they look in progress and can sometimes find this demoralising. Stick with it and trust the process.

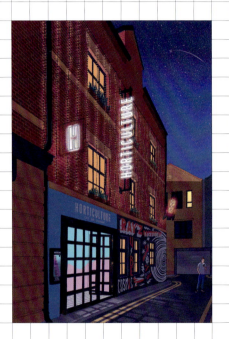

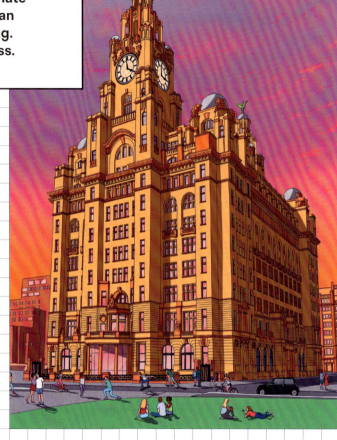

Experimenting with light is my favourite part of the illustration process – it brings work to life. If it helps with the composition, add in lampposts or light fittings where you need to.

Play around with different textures – there are loads of Procreate brush download resources online. Folio. procreate.art is a great resource for free brushes, or you can buy brush packs from Creative Market.

Yvette Earl

Step by Step

This illustration showcases older buildings and ornate details. I took a few photos and got started in **Procreate**. It's hard to get every detail in photos, so I often use Google Street View to zoom into buildings. I set up my artboards in RGB and convert to CMYK in Photoshop when setting up for print. Working with print products in mind, I set artboards at 300dpi and around 410 x 286mm, which leaves me 34–37 layers to work with and I can print up to A0 size with ease. **Procreate** layers and clipping masks allows you to move items around or delete and change as you go. The drawing takes me roughly the same time as colouring. Experimenting with textures and applying them to different colours by using clipping masks is a great part of the process. If you're unfamiliar, there are many tutorials online with tips and tricks.

Tools: Procreate, iPad, Apple Pencil

1.

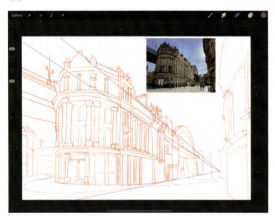

Use pencil brushes for the initial sketch in red. Layer up sketches in different colours with vanishing point lines for reference. Grid lines help to keep everything straight – they are found under 'Canvas', then turn 'Drawing Guide' on.

2.

Add in more detailed linework. Keep different elements in separate layers with contrasting colours to adjust with ease as needed.

3.

Use a fine-tip brush for linework, with different photo references on your canvas (this can be at least a full day's work).

4.

To save time where a part of a building repeats, draw the first part in, copy and paste this part as many times as required, then knock the transparency back and trace over these. It saves having to redraw every bit from scratch, and helps with perspective.

5.

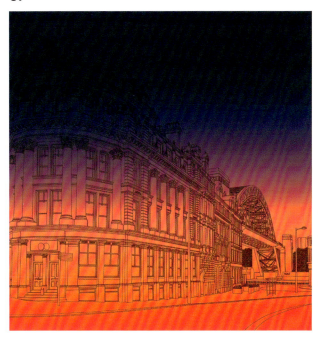

Getting into colouring, add the sky. Add in multiple different colours on top of each other in a layer, then use the blur option under 'Adjustments' to blend the colours together and create gradients.

6.

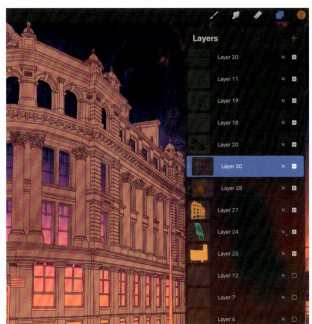

When colouring the elements, keep everything on separate layers so you can adjust colours if parts aren't working together. Apply all textures on separate layers, using clipping masks to mask them to the sections of colour.

7.

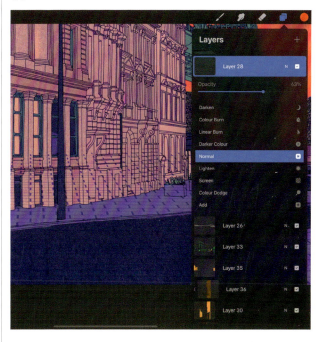

Use building pattern brushes to add a pavement pattern. Draw flat to start with, then use the Distort tool to adjust the perspective and apply the pattern using a clipping mask. Once the base colours are down, start working on any colours that need adjusting.

8.

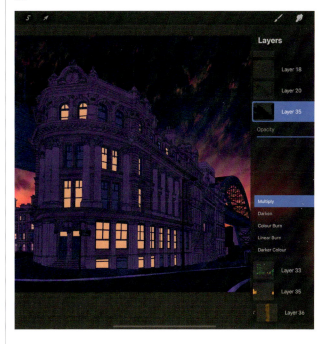

Add the shadows. I apply a full black layer over everything but the sky and the windows that are lit up. On the Layers panel blending options, I put this layer on 'Multiply' – I find this blends best with everything – then play around with the transparency and see what works.

9.

Adding a black layer all over makes it easier to erase the highlights back into it.

10.

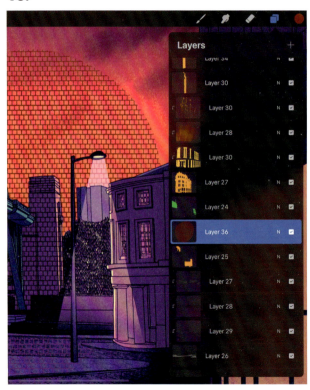

Work in smaller details, adding more brick patterns to the building using a brick brush. Add lamppost lighting by setting the Layers panel blending option to 'Linear Light'. Experiment with the blending options; each one works differently on every colour and texture. Add more lampposts if the drawing lacks light in the foreground.

11.

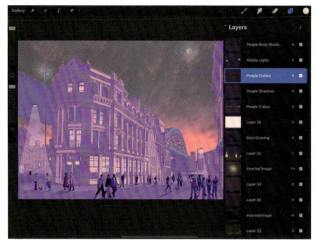

Add people on top of everything. These are a big part of the composition, so you need the ability to move them around; apply the white layer to see what you're drawing on top.

12.

To create the shadows on the floor, duplicate the colour layer and distort the perspective, then colour it black and knock the transparency down so it matches the rest of the shadows.

Yvette Earl

"Drawings lie ... or at least they tell us the untruths we want to hear ..."

Line Politics
Bryan Cantley

Title:
**Owner at Form:uLA
and Professor of
Design Theory, CSUF**

Instagram:
@bcantl3y

Story

Growing up in a very small farming community in rural North Carolina,
exposure to large farming machinery and oversized road-making
equipment pointed my graphic sensibilities to both the act of construction,
as well as the mechanical romanticism of these mobile utilitarian
architectures. Since the cultural atmosphere was thin in said rural
community, comic books – Jack Kirby and George Perez were huge –
and machine/appliance owner's manuals became my graphic retreat.
My techniques reflect the mechanical cleanness of these rich, but
often dismissed, media.

FIND ME:

Inspiration

I typically spend many hours in my sketchbooks chasing out conceptual structuring for my drawings. There is *always* a concept; a series of enquiries/pursuits that precedes any linework. The sketchbook format is beneficial to me as it allows for the development of diagramming and the evolution of the ideas via text. I always set up a series of rules and parameters before a drawing commences, and then I additionally allow numerous 'adaptive rulesets' to emerge and develop as the drawing advances. The sub-rules often provide the friction of conflict to the original rules. The work is incredibly organic in its structuring – there is no end product envisioned at the beginning. I have a philosophy of 'line politics' that explores the nature of friction and conflict resolution within the complexity of the composition.

Process

There are a plethora of techniques I employ depending on the drawing and/or its series/classification. Since I work primarily in analogue with a heavy digital research component, the techniques often evolve based on the conditions being created. The methods used are quite basic – pencil-drafted construction/massing lines, ink on Mylar/Dura-Lar linework, ink shadows, application of Zip-A-Tone as needed, then text/images applied as the last layer of media. Within that process there can be time manipulating digital components/imagery, more time in sketchbooks writing/thinking, and many layers of (yellow) tracing paper in between each of the 'layers of process'.

I adopted a philosophical stance of what I call 'live active layering' based on the introduction of **Photoshop** 'layers' in 1995, which opened up a new universe of how to deal with conceptual and physical layering. Instead of thinking of drawing as a singular physical event, this notion allowed for both the physical and the conceptual layers of a drawing to become active and rearrange themselves based on focus and shifting intentions/applications.

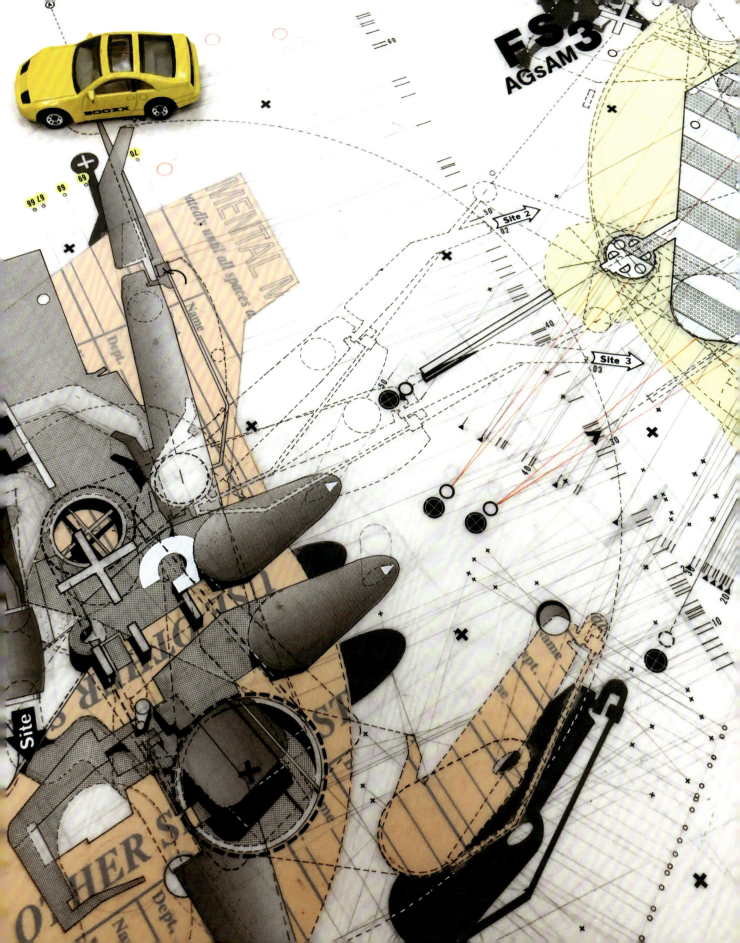

Tips

Ink mistakes are frequent and must be embraced/celebrated, as it is a non-forgiving medium – there is no 'delete' button on an ink drawing.

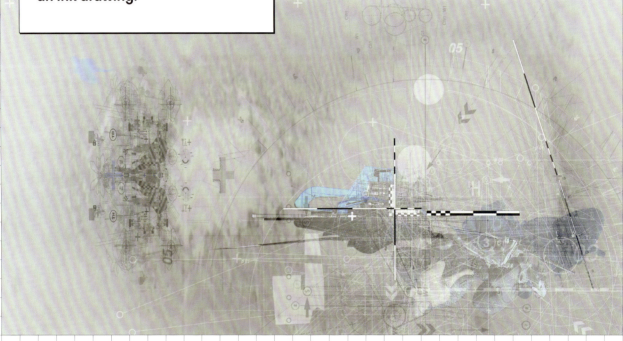

Drawings are considered fluid, meaning I make and read them as 'dynamic', as opposed to the static condition of most drawings.

Do not fear the unknown. Allow the act of drawing to be speculative and experimental – see where the drawing takes you, as opposed to where you may take it.

Dotted or dashed lines show not only position and movement, but also chronological and conceptual shifting.

Drawing Attention

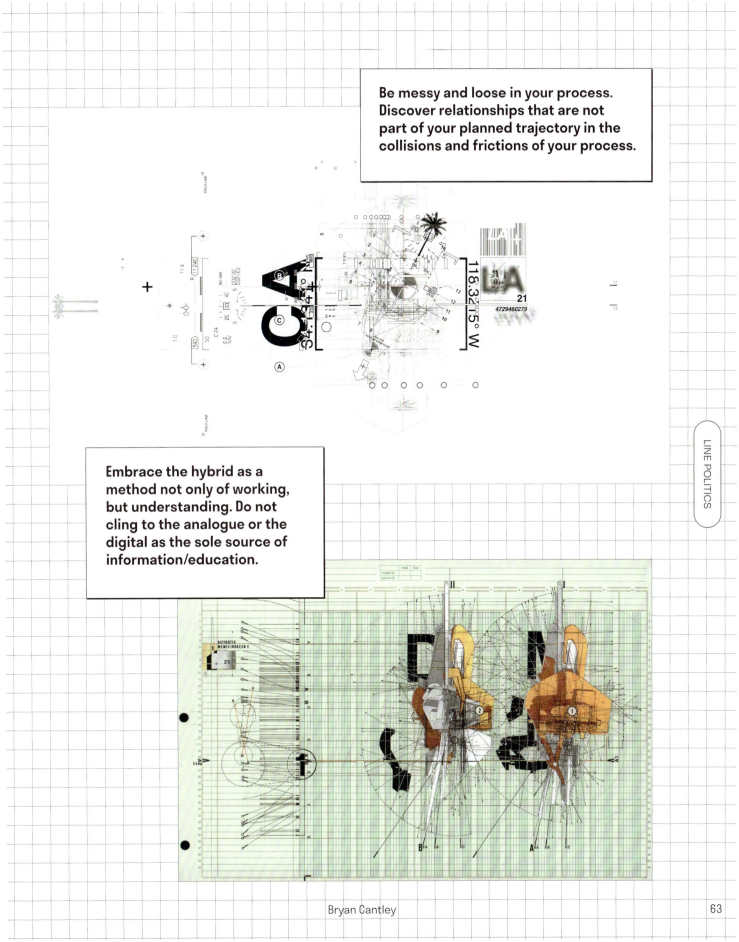

Be messy and loose in your process. Discover relationships that are not part of your planned trajectory in the collisions and frictions of your process.

Embrace the hybrid as a method not only of working, but understanding. Do not cling to the analogue or the digital as the sole source of information/education.

Bryan Cantley

Step by Step

This drawing started as a set of experiments exploring the inequities and accessibility within the architecture profession and discipline. I discovered quickly that getting into 'great schools' was not an option, as I was coming from a non-wealthy family from a rural area. I discovered that without access to said schools, it was challenging at best to find employment at the 'top firms'. The cycle repeats its condition of closing itself off to the non-elite. There emerged an idea of communications, or data of importance, being accessible to only a select few, hence the series' use of inter-office memo envelopes as the site of investigation. These formal and physical methods of communication were inherently exclusive, though they were passed around architecture offices within eyesight of anyone – almost flaunting the inaccessibility of critical data. The drawing, fourth or fifth in the series, expressed the frustrations of this exclusive openness of communication and denial. There is a compositional dialogue between the method of communication(s) on the left, and the product/discipline on the right of the drawing. The envelope is the field condition on the left side, blank cells from a ledger book representing the receptacle of that communication data on the right side. Formal dimensionalised masses anchor the left, while flat, un-massed drawing data occupy the right, which also receives the small shadow of the left-hand components as a blockage of possible (en)light(enment).

Tools: Graphite, vellum, mylar, Zip-A-Tone, X-Acto Blade, black ink, cellophane, white ink, transfer sheets, Photoshop

1.

Create the basic initial ground/base layer layout. Try traditional analogue drafting techniques, such as graphite on vellum. Inaugurate the major compositional figural relationships and massing politics. Establish figure/ground, and precincts/zones of spatial occupation will begin to emerge as the drawing develops.

2.

Establish the initial inking layer. Formal relations found between physical layers of multiple sheets of Mylar are constructed from early compositional and relational research.

3.

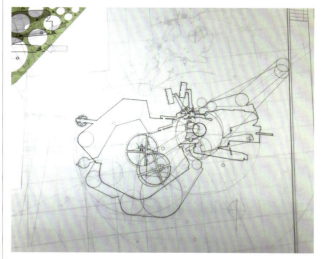

Add additional inking layers as the line politics interactions and conflicts between forms, spaces and linework and complex relationships begin evolving internal/external dialogues. Geometrical, geographical and chronological references develop their own notational systems. Allow each system in the drawing to develop their own notational structures, thus creating new opportunities when they collide.

4.

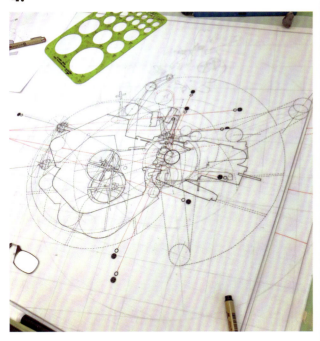

Notational structures emerge as contributors to the dialogue. Projection mapping continues to evolve as the drawings' rules and parameters are expanded. Inking occurs in multiple layers and colours, delineating the occupancy potential of each zone.

6.

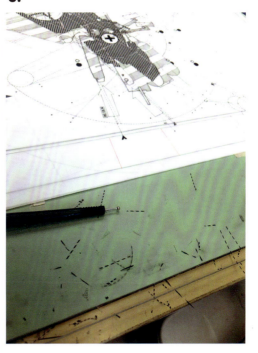

Draw dotted lines by hand, as well as with a knife via appliqué transfer sheets, which requires surgical precision. Lines are dimensional and behave as such, making them particularly challenging to corral.

5.

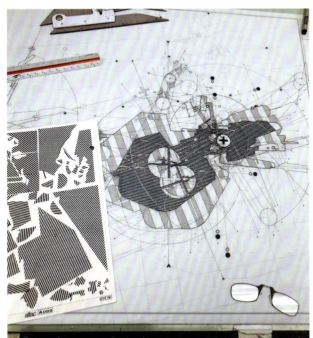

Zones of occupancy, cross-references and emergent zones are born, here shown to be designated by Zip-A-Tone application. Drawing with an X-Acto blade is as critical as drawing with a pen, as the appliqué membranes are hand cut and applied on top of the ink layer.

7.

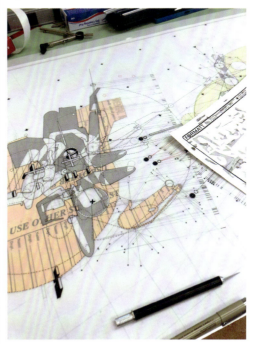

Shading by careful drawing with the knife extracts intimate and complex shapes to assign to specified volumes/massings. Spatial thickness is suggestive in this type of drawing, mimicking a 3D-modelled environment. Rapidograph and Micron pens are used for inking masses.

8.

(Back)masking is a technique of cutting/shaping solid/semi-solid shapes to be attached to the back of the Mylar sheet. This gives a sense of depth of field that is difficult to achieve if all graphic impregnation is on the same physical level. Here, brown memo envelopes and yellow cellophane determine the two voices in the drawing conversation.

9.

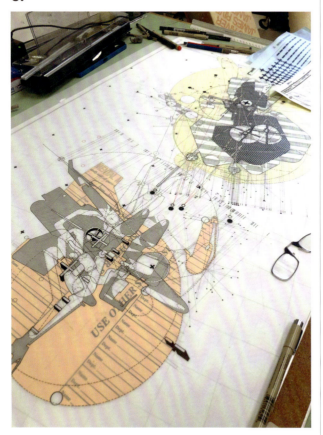

Use transfer sheets to establish repetitive graphic notations. These are typically the last layer to occur, as the media is now defunct (for 15 years) and very unstable. Any work done to the surface typically removes such notations, hence it being one of the last steps.

10.

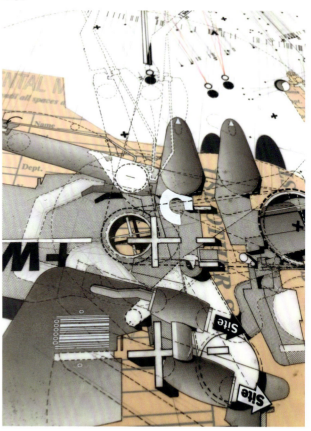

Hand-augment white transfers using white ink to adjust surface discrepancies when applying transfers on top of transfers. Re-inking/adjusting is quite common due to the fragility and lack of fidelity of such aged media.

11.

Take the final drawing for a test spin to make sure all bolts have been tightened to specifications before unveiling.

Tighten background, calibrate colours, shine shoes.

"Drawing is relentless tranquillity exercised to conceal vacancy."

Digital Art
Malavika Madhuraj

Title:
**MS Advanced Architectural
Design Student at Columbia
University, New York**

Instagram:
@lost___lab

Story

Being an artist is straining on the cusp of an unuttered yearning of
creation while momentarily lapsing into a reverie of hesitation. I was never
formally trained in drawing, but being an architecture student meant
I had to cross with drawings eventually. At first, I mostly practised with
graphite pencils, coloured pencils, charcoal, pastels and watercolours,
but I soon began rehearsing with other mediums such as digital art.

Transitioning from traditional mediums to digital wasn't as easy
as I expected; it relies on a different skillset than its conventional
counterparts. For a while, I accepted that my hands were just
programmed for tangible paper and pen. Usually, when I am drawing and
assume it will turn out terribly midway, I have the strongest inclination to
stop and abandon it. However, working digitally, we have the adaptability
to experiment with layers and erase mistakes. The ability of this medium
to circumvent the hesitation that springs from the indelibility and
permanence associated with drawing on paper has made a big difference
for me.

FIND ME:

Inspiration

I believe beyond the design of buildings as products. Every cross-section, material choice and concept drawing engages in the art of placemaking, revising and reframing the references of a place. As an architecture student, I end up behind my screen for an extended period. While I have discovered heaps of visual inspiration through online journals and web-based media sites, I'm usually most enlivened when I step away from my screen.

Inspiration can come from the most random things – a flick of a book, an unlit corridor, cracks on the wall, gnarled tree roots, heat of the night. What you are looking for is often already around you.

Putting even your most embryonic concepts and thoughts on paper can lend clarity to them. Even when you are not actively looking for an idea, it's beneficial to keep a sketchbook with you to record whenever possible.

Process

Drawing ought to bring out an idea, a memory or a thought. In digital art, it is easy to get caught up with the extensive set of brushes and apparatuses, bouncing from one to another before growing fully comfortable with the one you started with.

Similarly, don't get too reliant on Ctrl+Z [undo], assuming your fingers are continually on that easy route. That dependency on the capacity to fix can hurt your results and your learning.

To navigate the digital space, I make a sketch in the traditional way first, then scan it, and add the embellishment and shading through a tablet. Over time, I've become more acquainted with the setup. There are many astounding works online; however, too much browsing can give you a negative view of your own progress. It's important to be patient with yourself and focus on building your fundamentals.

Tips

Mixing tones is fundamental to making a smooth, three-dimensional impact. There are numerous ways of doing this, with soft-edge brush, smearing device and blender brush being the most well-known instruments. Pick your strategy depending on the impact you are hoping to accomplish.

Start off your drawing process by outlining the volumes. The most complex structures can often be separated into fundamental geometric articles.

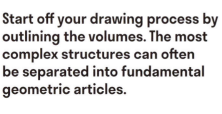

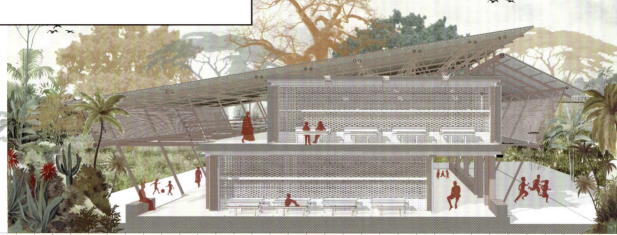

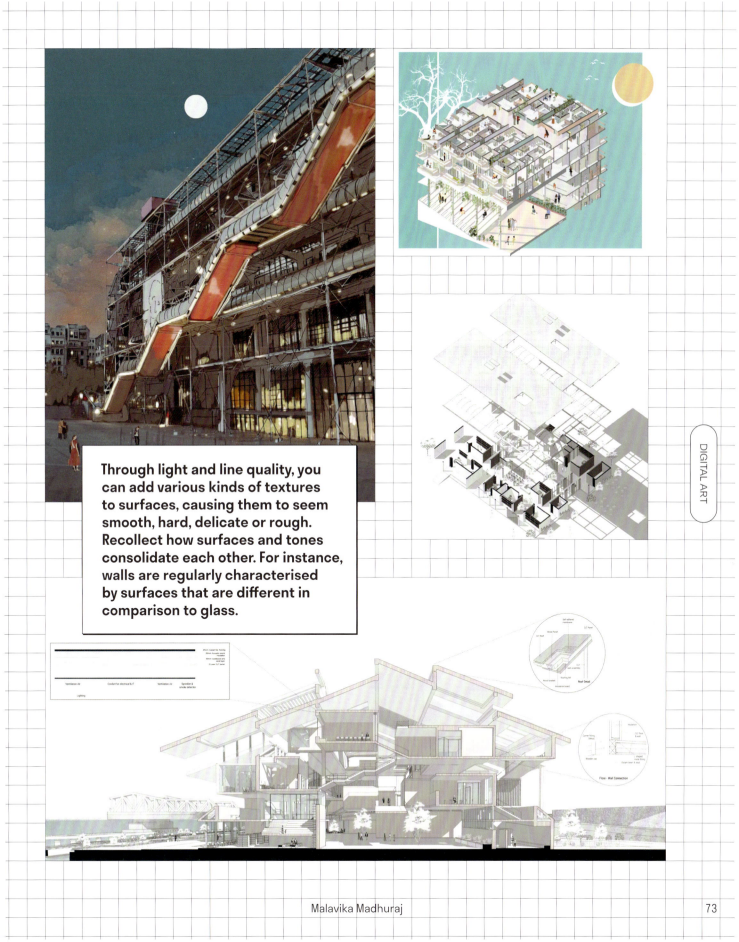

Through light and line quality, you can add various kinds of textures to surfaces, causing them to seem smooth, hard, delicate or rough. Recollect how surfaces and tones consolidate each other. For instance, walls are regularly characterised by surfaces that are different in comparison to glass.

Malavika Madhuraj

Step by Step

Like skyscrapers and yellow taxis, fire escapes are synonymous with New York. They are a quintessential piece of the city's scene, used for a spot to sit outside, to wrap articles of clothing around to dry, even to foster a couple of plants. Having moved here recently for graduate studies, it felt fitting for me to make a drawing of something ubiquitous in the city. Moreover, I wanted to capture how this iron ivy could become the remnant of an industrial age.

While making the drawing, there is a visual structure or hierarchy that focuses in on a part or series of parts in your drawing. This method is used here to provide noticeable weight to some components. This hierarchy permits you to focus on specific parts of the drawing. There is also a layering in play, where the stairs are overdrawn and placed on the top to allude to depth. Layering can likewise be identified with shading, linework or how you contemplate lightness.

Sometimes, it's the subtleties and details of a drawing that best show your comprehension of surface, scale and light. This can mean the exacting subtleties of a structure or development, or how a drawing is executed at numerous scales.

Tools: SketchBook, Illustrator, Photoshop, Procreate

1.

Sketch out the drawing and frame it within the canvas you have in mind. Making quick outlines with thin brushes assists me with zooming in on the process rather than the end result. Sketching in this relaxed manner provides a space to explore the topic without having any expectations of the final product.

2.

Try **Procreate** or **SketchBook** using an **Apple Pencil**. Edit your canvas size and decide on the orientation and scale of your drawing in the settings. Start filling in random strokes and linework to add depth to the drawing.

3.

Colours can rejuvenate a drawing. There are three fundamental classifications of colourisation: highly contrasting drawings which are black and white, drawings with a couple of colours, or a whole-colour delivery. In greyscale, you just show lines with different thicknesses, notwithstanding shade and shadow. In picking a couple of colours, you can zero in on the lines or individual components.

Flip your material or pivot your model while working in 3D. You may see something you need to fix or change that wasn't noticeable from your previous perspective. Layers allow you to separate components of your drawing for control and impact – moving, gathering, changing and mixing them to construct your drawing.

DIGITAL ART

Consider light functions to make your drawing three-dimensional. A careful treatment of light, shadow and tone can assist with defining the frame. Add people to give your drawing more character.

For final touches, import the drawing into **Photoshop** and work on the post-processing. Add text and typography. You can also use **Photoshop** layers and masks to add and strengthen textures. Subtle adjustments can make a huge difference in the perception of the image.

The Basics of Healthy Productivity
Sana Tabassum

Title:
Founder of :scale

Instagram:
@to.scale

The path to unlocking creative confidence and passion for design projects often comes at the cost of sleep and the social lives of students, no matter the year of study or even the country. Although this is an incredibly common phase that almost all architecture students go through, the current generation is facing a shift in mindset which redefines the meaning of being productive. It isn't always easy to churn out incredibly complicated drawings that tick all the boxes, because you're already bombarded with so many other deadlines and tasks.

By unpacking processes and identifying smarter and healthier ways of working used by entrepreneurs and successful individuals from other disciplines, you can achieve high standards without burnout. Here are a few pointers that may help you as a student .

1. Set boundaries and treat university work like a nine-to-five job, working within set hours with regular breaks. Perhaps architecture students will finally be able to stop obsessing over productivity once they realise it is possible to find a good balance between life and university work simply through enjoying the journey as much as the output.
2. Pull from the media you consume, such as films, literature or even music to supplement the interests and passions you already have and showcase these throughout your work. This is a great way of channelling your energy and creativity while also having fun. This can allow you to maximise your research, which is crucial. A solid foundation of research will help strengthen your project narrative, acting as the backbone for further exploration.

FIND ME:

3. Finding your optimum energy period during the day will benefit you in designing a routine and habit that you are comfortable with. But be very careful to balance out working hours with time to recharge and step away from university work. Regardless of whether you are a night owl or an early bird, work accordingly to whichever feels easiest.

4. Be realistic with yourself. It's easy to get lost in the drawings you work on, so try to be strict and set yourself deadlines or assign a handful of tasks per day to keep a healthy flow of activities. Most students fail to gauge this easily, so having friends and peers to hold you accountable can also help. It goes without saying that spending the right amount of time will increase the quality of your work, but try not to overdo this in the name of all-nighters. Sleep is the most important factor when it comes to a healthy lifestyle.

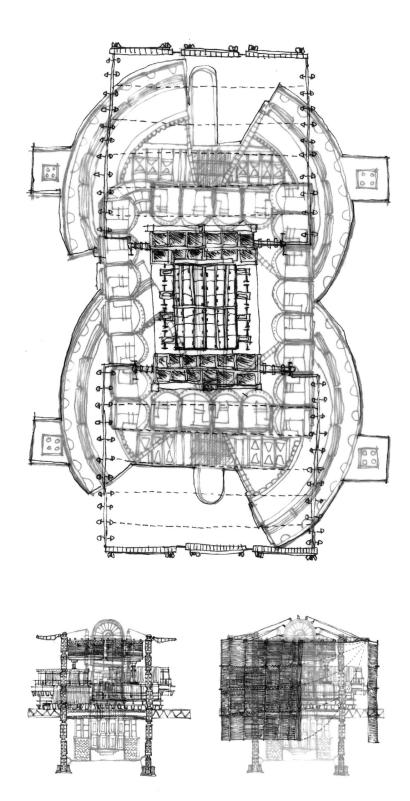

Drawing Attention

"Look at precedents to avoid what has been done before."

Architecture Anomaly
Saul Kim Min Kyu

Title:
**Harvard Graduate School of
Design, creator of Architecture
Anomaly series, creator and host
of Random Thoughts podcast,
instructor at Domestika**

Instagram:
@saul_kim_

Story

Architecture Anomaly is an ongoing design study series I started in
2020. It can be seen as a personal design catalogue that documents my
experimentations with form and space. I try to draw inspiration from
the silliest things, like discarded cardboard boxes, bent paperclips
and tangled wires. My works are essentially architectural objects that
are liberated from the pragmatic issues of architecture. Hence, they
have no sense of context and scale. The only purpose of the study is to
express my ideas through architectural forms. I'm a strong believer in
'design over-representation', which means that I would first prioritise the
product of design and later figure out how to represent it in the most
literal way possible: no colours, no collage and no labels that serve a
graphical purpose. I would consider my drawing skills rudimentary, and
this is because I honestly do not have an innate interest in architectural
representation techniques. However, I believe it is the simplicity and the
directness of my representation that help convey my ideas to a larger
audience in the clearest way.

FIND ME:

Inspiration

The concept of my drawing is about generating the purest expressions of abstract ideas. I always think of my design as a thing in itself, which relates to the idea of *noumena*. In other words, the focus is only on the object, which should be studied independently of human perception. Hence, I avoid adding things that would give specificity to the drawing. The drawings should present themselves as abstract ideas with potential for development, but not as predefined architectural projects. I achieve this by removing the pragmatic elements of architecture, such as context and material. Once I start to add recognisable and realistic materials such as brick, this gives away the scale and the logic of construction. This would prevent me from having room for different kinds of interpretation as to how the idea might be developed into an architectural project.

Process

For my drawing, I use **Rhino 3D** for modelling and **V-Ray** for rendering. Because this is an ongoing design study series, the number of projects increases day by day. To keep a consistent format throughout the series, I decided to create a default drawing style consisting of four main elements. First, a seamless ground plane that is white and slightly reflective. This gives a backdrop to the overall drawing. It also has no colour, because it has no defined materiality. The second element is the architectural object, positioned in the centre of the drawing as the focus. I often use concrete texture to create a juxtaposition between the object and the ground plane. Cast-in-place concrete is a material that can be used at a variety of scales without subdivision, from full-scale buildings to small-scale architectural models. Therefore the materiality, in this case, does not specify the scale of the object. It can be interpreted as both a full-scale building and a small-scale model. For the third element, human scale figures are placed on the object. They suggest the usable spaces and the activities that could take place within the object. Just like the ground plane, the material of the human scale figures remains undefined. Lastly, the soft lighting gives the drawing a studio-like ambience. The shadow cast on both the object itself and the ground plane gives depth to the overall drawing. These four elements are the most basic yet essential components in my drawings, as they allow for both abstraction and clarity.

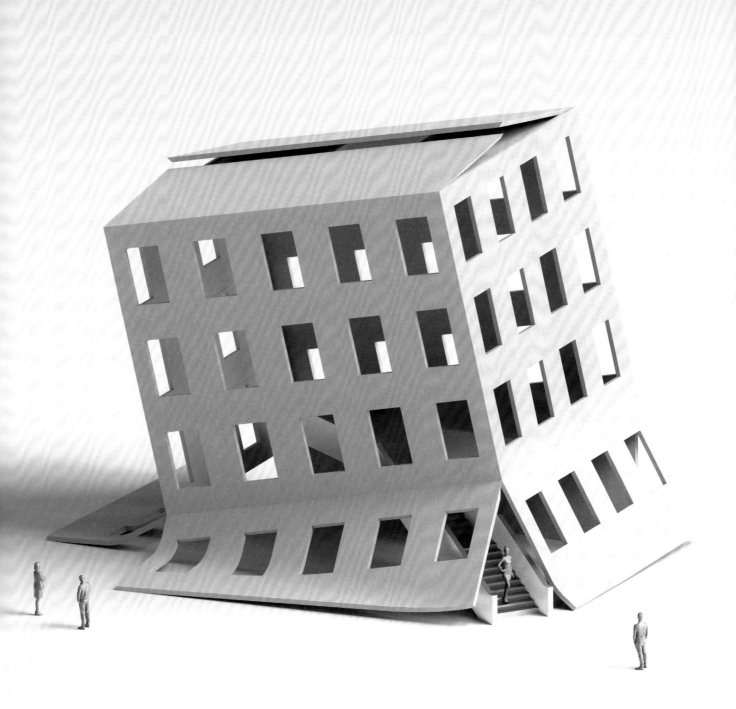

Tips

Always put human figures in both the interior and exterior spaces of the project.

It is crucial to design with recognisable architectural elements, because they serve as the preconceived conventions of architecture. They are formally manipulated afterwards to create anomalous juxtapositions.

Drawing Attention

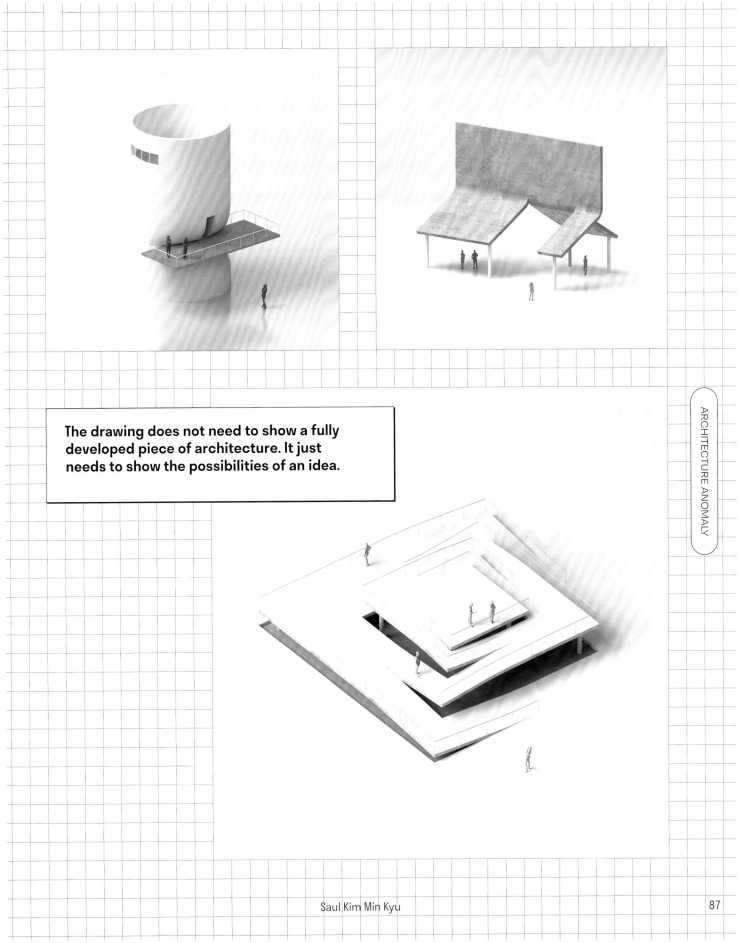

The drawing does not need to show a fully developed piece of architecture. It just needs to show the possibilities of an idea.

Step by Step

'Conformity' is the study of ways in which parts come together. At a minimum, two pieces or things need to be present for the interaction. The only rule here is to not follow the rule of conventional assembly of architecture. The project is made with simple and recognisable elements, such as a truss and a mound. The familiarity of these elements serves as the set-up for juxtaposition and contradiction. When we see these recognisable parts, they trigger the preconceived notion of how they normally look and how they're normally used and what they're normally used for. Ordinary and banal elements can turn into spectacles with transposition and manipulation. The manipulation and misappropriation of these elements creates something that is almost surrealistic and anomalous, defying spatial and formal conventions of architecture.

There was an interest in making the ground an architectural element, applying to it the same knowledge and technique of conformity. It is a juxtaposition between ground and truss; one that operates with a grid system and repetition, and the other that operates autonomously. Through the way in which the architecture here 'lands' on the ground – or rather, not 'lands', but 'fits' – to levitate in the air, it passes its role of structure and circulation to the ground, empowering the ground to do more than it normally would.

There are two essential design rules here. One: the ground must smoothly deviate from the environment to be seen as a continuous plane. Two: the architecture needs to remain in the most primitive shape possible (a box). This allows for the two elements to appear contradictory, generating an unusual formal experience.

Tools: Hand-drawing, Rhino 3D, V-Ray

1.

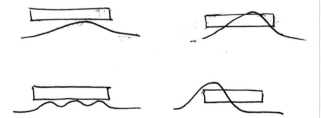

It starts with a simple question: what if the ground could levitate the architecture? Here, I begin by creating basic sectional diagrams which explore how the two elements (ground and mass) can become one. The concept could also be described as 'constant versus autonomous', and so these quick initial pen drawings are a way to test ideas and decide the concept.

2.

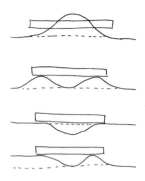

It is helpful to record the chronology of design ideas to create as many options as possible. The more you iterate, the better the idea gets; start early, work fast and rough. This step shows the diagrams developing not just in their maturity of concept, but also the introduction of a new line type (dashed) to indicate 'real ground', as the previous ground has now become an architectural/structural element.

3.

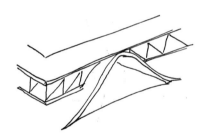

Test the idea with reference to structural expression and solidity. Doing so in sketch form will help you decide whether more conceptual development is needed before 3D modelling in **Rhino**, ultimately saving time and making the process more efficient.

4.

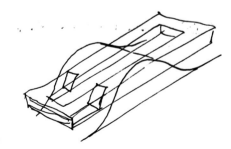

Here, I realise that the concept does require further development and I make a design decision to bring the ground plane all the way up into the mass to intersect with it.

5.

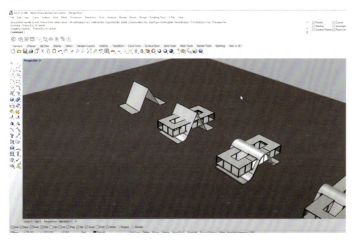

3D modelling requires you to find solutions. I start with a simplified version of my geometry to build the crude beginnings of my design. This step shows a sharp surface I created by simply extruding a polyline in **Rhino** that intersects with a basic rectangular mass.

6.

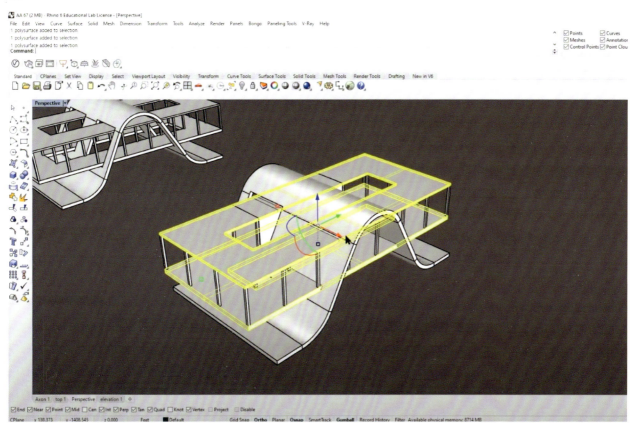

Simple **Rhino** commands can help to achieve your concept. You must see your model as a combination of simple geometry, and usually basic commands will do the trick. To achieve a curve, try 'FilletEdge' on the sharp extruded polyline corners, which is quicker and more accurate than trying to draw a symmetrical curve and extruding it.

7.

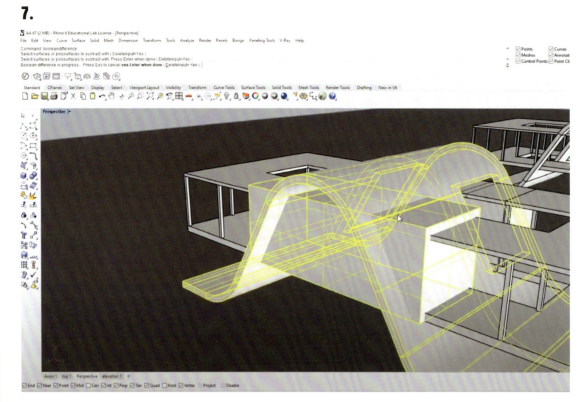

Here, I use the **Rhino** command 'Intersect' while selecting the rectangular horizontal planes and the oscillating 'ground' to reveal the edges of their intersections. I use those intersections to create a box using the 'BoundingBox' command. This box fits perfectly in the junctions between my masses.

8.

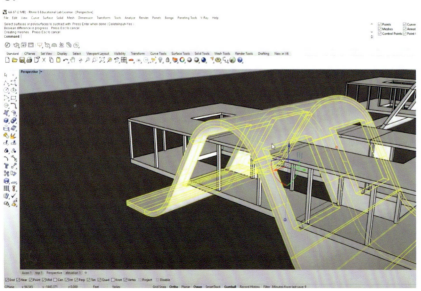

Now I offset the box using the 'OffsetSrf' command and use the 'BooleanDifference' command to subtract the box from the masses, revealing an offset void. This creates a loose-fitting effect, which exaggerates the design concept by creating more distinction between the two elements.

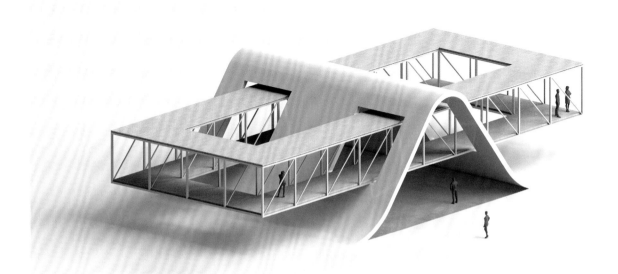

The design study is completed by selecting materials to achieve the desired effect. Having viewed the structure as an object, a metallic ground material made it possible to cast shadows and create reflections, which highlighted it as an object in focus. I chose a concrete material for the oscillating mass, which expressed the structure, and a plain white material for the rectangular platform to create a juxtaposition.

"To draw is to (re)invent memories."

Mega Drawings
Ana Aragão

Title:
Founder, Ana Aragão Atelier, Porto

Instagram:
@anaaragao

Story

I studied architecture in Porto, where drawing plays an extremely important role in the course. The intense six-year journey laid the path to my illustration life, which I only discovered when I was doing my PhD. I started to draw during classes and my colleagues started to ask me about the drawings, which is when I discovered my language: drawing projects by hand. From there, I decided to quit the PhD and make a living from drawing; it can be challenging, but it is rewarding to do what I love. I appreciate the rigour of architectural drawings, exploring perspective and mostly details. I am also fascinated by maps and encoded representations.

FIND ME:

Inspiration

The concepts of my drawings come from eclectic places: a section of a book, an image, a city, another artist or a place. Some examples: a series of drawings called *hronir*, exhibited in one of my solo shows in Macau, comes from two books written by the Argentinian master Jorge Luis Borges. The association of the ideas contained in the short story 'Tlön, Uqbar, Orbis Tertius' (in *Fictions*), and the *Book of Imaginary Beings* originated a collection of small watercolour and pen drawings. Sometimes I reinterpret historical artworks that intrigue me, for example *The Tower of Babel* by Pieter Bruegel the Elder, which I drew with a BIC pen in a large-scale format; *Idea delle antiche vie Appia e Ardeatina* by Giovanni Battista Piranesi, which I reinterpreted in terms of content and transformed in a printed glass installation; and *Città Ideale* by Fra Carnevale, which I rearranged with my personal view of architectural references. Drawing is a way of memorising things that touch us and that we don't want to lose.

Process

Techniques I use regularly include pen (Pilot 0.4 or Micron) on white paper and BIC pen on yellowish backdrop paper. I usually draw directly with a pen, making a few pencil lines underneath, but I also like to explore new techniques, such as watercolour, coloured pencils or collage. In a recent exhibition on Japan, I tried to apply watercolour, but it was not working on the paper I wanted, so I explored coloured pencils for the first time. Once I figured out the potential, it was exciting to explore and try out gradients. You have to be open to adapting the process and technique with fluidity to achieve the best possible outcome. Errors are a key part of the process. It is important to have a safe place in terms of technique and methodology, but let the paths vary.

Ana Aragão

Tips

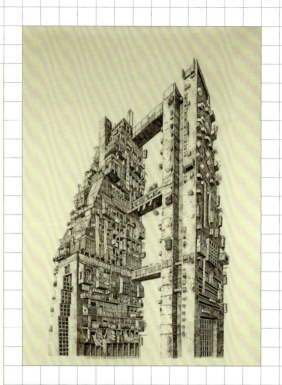

Use only one colour with the aim of giving meaning to the composition.

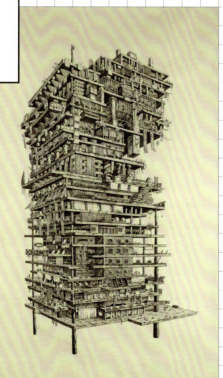

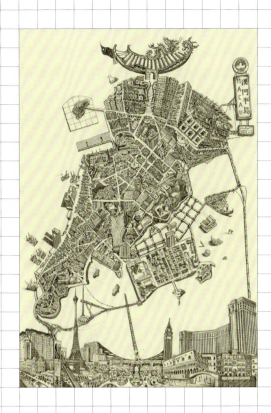

Draw as if it were your first and last drawing.

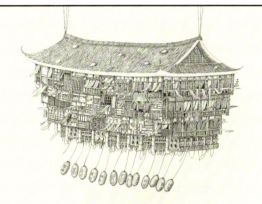

Try drawing on the floor with your body over the material; be patient, physically resistant and change your body position regularly.

Ana Aragão

Step by Step

The idea of the drawing was to reinterpret Bruegel the Elder's Tower of Babel, dated c.1563. Urban myths, megastructures and images of built density are fascinating. *The Tower of Babel* is the epitome of the majestic megastructure. The biblical narrative talks about a great tower of mutual understanding that would reach the sky, and of how God decided to confuse the languages so that men dispersed over the surface of the earth. All the megastructures, imagined by architects throughout time, have this common genealogy. I am profoundly interested in megastructures (Boullée, Piranesi, Buckminster Fuller, Le Corbusier, Archigram, Archizoom, the Japanese Metabolists, Koolhaas and so many other main characters in architectural history); in the idea of a physical structure that can contain everyone and everything, like a world globe. Although impossible, it is one of the most poetic and frightening ideas for solving the city and the dichotomy of vertical density versus horizontal/land spreading. My Babel is charged with a certain negativity and weight, unlike many of my other drawings, that lean towards lightness. It is my critical reading of present times. The process was tough, taking several months on two paper sheets, but the technique was simple, with only black BIC pen on paper. I spent the whole day on the floor drawing it. I usually work from the top to the bottom; this time I made it like an architect, from the bottom to the top.

Tools: Hand drawn

1.

Make a rough sketch of the idea. The sketch provides a mental and graphic reference throughout the whole work. In this case, I am reinterpreting the famous painting by Bruegel the Elder, of the Babel Tower. If the drawing works well in a five-minute sketch, it will likely work on a bigger scale.

2.

Start the final drawing, filling the sheet with seemingly infinite black pen lines. If it is a large drawing – say 150 cm x 200 cm – divide it across two separate sheets of paper. Try using only two drawing materials. In this drawing, I only use a pencil (a few lines for the outline) and a black BIC pen.

3.

Start to draw the background using your imagination, with just an initial historical image as reference. Think of it as a live process and let the drawing take you where it wants to go. Depending on the size, the result could take weeks or months. Here, I start to draw the background, namely everything that is around the Babel Tower.

4

Try to draw lying down on the floor over the drawing. It requires great concentration and careful body movement, so that the drawing doesn't get damaged; there is no room for mistakes, as the pen is not erasable. Get up and look at the drawing from a distance to get a complete perspective. Sometimes I spend the whole day lying on the floor.

5.

Set a defined end point. The finishing of a drawing is more of a mental decision than a graphic one. Actively take the decision that the drawing is finished, because, in theory, you could keep retouching forever. My black and white version of the Babel Tower recalls a dystopia that reminds us of the impossibility of living together in peace and reaching the same goals (the sky).

MEGA DRAWINGS

Reflect on the final drawing once it is finished. Drawings such as these do not have to be for a commission or a special project, but are a way to externalise unsayable feelings and emotions. There is no need for a message beyond the observer's interpretation. Once finished, the drawing belongs to the observer, to the world. Detach yourself from it to start a new project. An unfinished drawing haunts you; a finished drawing frees you.

"Regardless of skill, sketching could be the best form of communication."

Drawing is Design
Salmaan Mohamed

Title:
Freelance architect and interior designer, content creator at Maan Meraki

Instagram:
@maan.meraki

Story

Through architecture, I found my way into sketching and I love the art of it. One of the biggest hurdles was stopping myself from chasing perfection and setting unrealistic standards. Overcoming this mental block is key. My journey truly began when I stopped trying to hide mistakes, as opposed to making everything look flawless and untainted – embrace the joy of the natural process of creation.

I enjoyed hand sketches but soon discovered digital sketching and fell in love with it too. People shouldn't be afraid of sketching. I try to showcase how it can be used as a tool to communicate ideas and emotions in the simplest way possible. My style is free-flowing, which can be seen in the organic, wavering lines.

FIND ME:

Inspiration

The difference between an artistic drawing and a design drawing is the underlying idea or 'concept'. The process of incorporating a concept into a drawing adds more value and meaning. A quote from architect Edmund Bacon says 'it's in the doing that the idea comes', and for me, the concept of a sketch develops as I create the thumbnail sketches or rough drafts. I try to keep it simple and straightforward, going back to basics such as contrast, scale and proportion as the guiding principles to emphasise the various elements in the drawing. What can help create strong concepts in a drawing is to refrain from overthinking and build on the elements that feature in your artwork.

Process

I primarily use three techniques: fully hand drawn, hand drawn plus digital, or completely digital. The choice of technique is based on my understanding of which can best bring out the nuances in a context. A hand sketch works best for quick sketches; a fusion of hand sketch plus digital works to highlight specifics in a sketch; and a digital sketch is effective for interior design presentations or large-scale drawings with multiple elements.

Each technique follows the same underlying process, starting with brainstorming ideas and creating thumbnail sketches to narrow down to the best possible composition. At this point I develop a vision of what the final outcome will look like, and the detailing begins.

Having multiple methodologies to create drawings is helpful, but it is good to practice to master one technique before taking on another.

Tips

To bring a particular area into focus, try scanning or photographing one part of your drawing and then digitally colouring it in Photoshop.

If you take a simple photo of a floor plan and then skew it in Photoshop you can use this as a guide for drawing with accurate perspective scale.

Step by Step

In the following illustration, we want to establish a connection between the indoors and the outdoors of an urban environment in an unconventional style, using techniques that are simple yet effective to convey the intent. The process begins with a flurry of hand sketches until one such hand sketch is finalised, scanned and imported into **Photoshop**. Once there, I will work out the best possible angle and colour palette before moving on to 3D modelling and spatial planning in **SketchUp**. The aim is to combine varying line weights coupled with multiple layers of yellow hues to create a lighting effect that is popular in the age of social media and will draw the viewer's attention. Finally, the addition of living beings and interior details will breathe life and story into the illustration. Adding a backdrop that includes different stages of structural evolution will help to give a city its signature look and iconic skyline.

Tools: Sketchup, Photoshop, Illustrator

1.

Create a drawing which reflects an indoor-outdoor environment after multiple sketches. The context of the sketch, the angle of view and possible elements can be added. Try highlighting the indoor environment with colour.

2.

Recreate the finalised hand sketch in **Photoshop** to get an idea of colours and how the elements will look when put together digitally. Use a stylus and a digital tablet to develop a vision of the final outcome.

3.

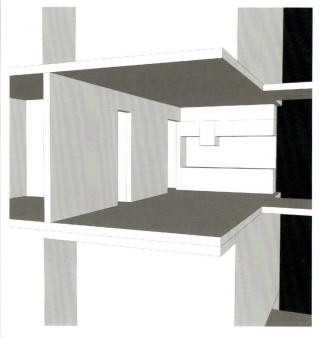

Devise a floor plan for the apartment and make a model in **SketchUp** to get the spatial arrangement for the concept. Once the angle of view has been decided, export it as an image into **Photoshop** to begin with the digital sketch.

4.

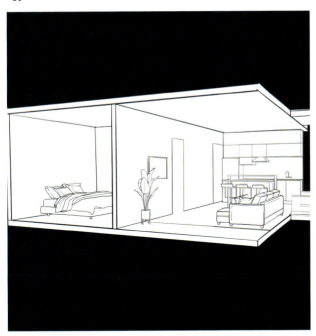

Use the exported base image to build the outlines of the space, furniture and accessories. It's best to have a range of line weights, creating outlines that give a sense of depth within the composition.

5.

Create the background with buildings at contrasting scales, with the smaller historical residences in the centre and skyscrapers along the outer edges. Make the outlines with a lighter line weight than the apartment in the foreground, and accentuate this with a grainy texture overlay to give the impression that they're far back in the composition.

6.

Reflect the minimal contemporary interior design style with an appropriate palette. Overlay each part of the interior with materials; textures that are further enhanced with shadows. Use hues of warm yellow to create light effects on the ceiling. Change the outline colours on each element to merge with the object.

7.

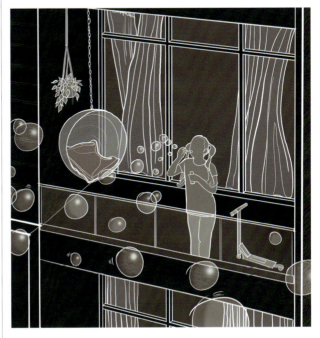

Enliven the form of the residence by creating a story about the inhabitants of the space. The resident of the main apartment space is a dog lover, and the neighbours downstairs are a family with two kids. Balcony space on each apartment varies according to the storyline.

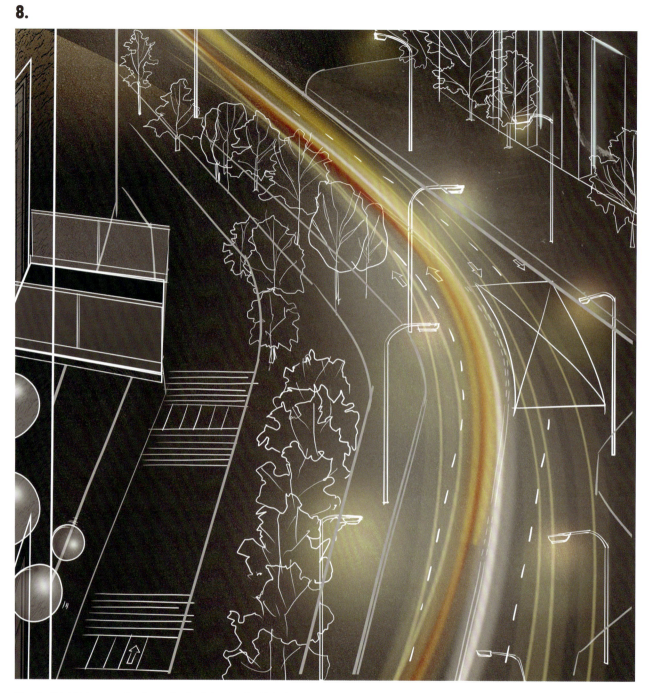

8

A touch of highlights can really enhance the details in a drawing. Light the streetlamps and a trail of traffic lights to create a point of interest in the roads. Give the buildings in the background a faint light effect through the windows to make them seem livelier.

The resulting drawing conveys information about context, location and spatial planning on an architectural level, as well as the relationship the inhabitants have with the space on an emotional level. The contrast of light and dark tones draws the eye towards the focal point of the apartment interior. A hierarchy of light effects from the foreground to distant buildings in the background adds depth to the composition.

Multimedia Representation
Thomas Rowntree

Title:
YouTuber, podcast host

YouTube:
ThomasRowntree

Architecture representation usually takes the form of a 2D static drawing; however, there are many other ways to communicate an idea. Students use sketchbooks, tracing paper, A2 pin-up sheets and models to express ideas because they are taught that this is the easiest and most accurate way to present their thinking. However, throughout my time studying, I found that multimedia representation provided me with a combination of design tools and methods of communication, which helped me explain my projects. Blending traditional and digital modes of representation can really help bring a narrative to life. New technology and software can unlock new representation methods. Mixed-media techniques utilising layering, cutting, editing and superimposing, can turn a drawing into an animation, or a render into a video or a 3D model into a walkthrough experience. Below are three suggestions for multimedia architectural representation.

Video
Video overlay can bring drawings to life. Filming models, spaces and drawings and editing them together as a mixed-media video can effectively describe your thinking. By superimposing drawings in a video editor such as Premiere Pro with footage of models, animated diagrams and even site photos, you are able to communicate complex information simultaneously. The techniques of montage editing, continuous editing and jump-cut edits can communicate speed, time and activity. This type of video editing can dramatically influence mood, activity and the rhythm of the spaces you are designing. Furthermore, audio can further enhance the atmosphere and ambience. Remember, filming and documenting the process of site visits, model-making and drawing may become useful at the later stages of a project to help explain the design steps taken. Always record as much as you can.

FIND ME:

Audio

Audio is a powerful tool to give enhanced context to drawings and models. Adding a soundtrack to a still image is a powerful storytelling device to add another dimension to your representations. To set the scene of your drawings you can add sound effects as well as atmospheric sounds. This helps place the viewer in the scene of a project and gives them cues on how they could feel in that space. Even narration can aid the explanation of a drawing or project to the viewers if you struggle to explain things during a crit. The combination and overlaying of dialogue, sound effects and atmospheric sounds can give your project the multisensory boost it needs.

Animation

Animation can be quite intimidating; however, a simple sequence to show the construction of a drawing and model can be very successful. You can film timelapses and stop-motion animations as short-form videos to explain the process of construction or the components of your proposal. Another simple animation technique is to use Photoshop's Timeline feature to show the activity of people and moving components within a floor plan, elevation, section or any other type of drawing. Multimedia representation does not have to be a complex operation.

The [frame]
Concept model

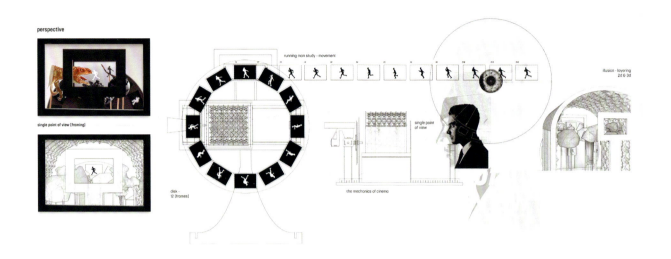

perspective

single point of view [framing]

running man study - movement

disk -
12 [frames]

single point
of view

the mechanics of cinema

illusion - layering
2d & 3d

STEP INSIDE

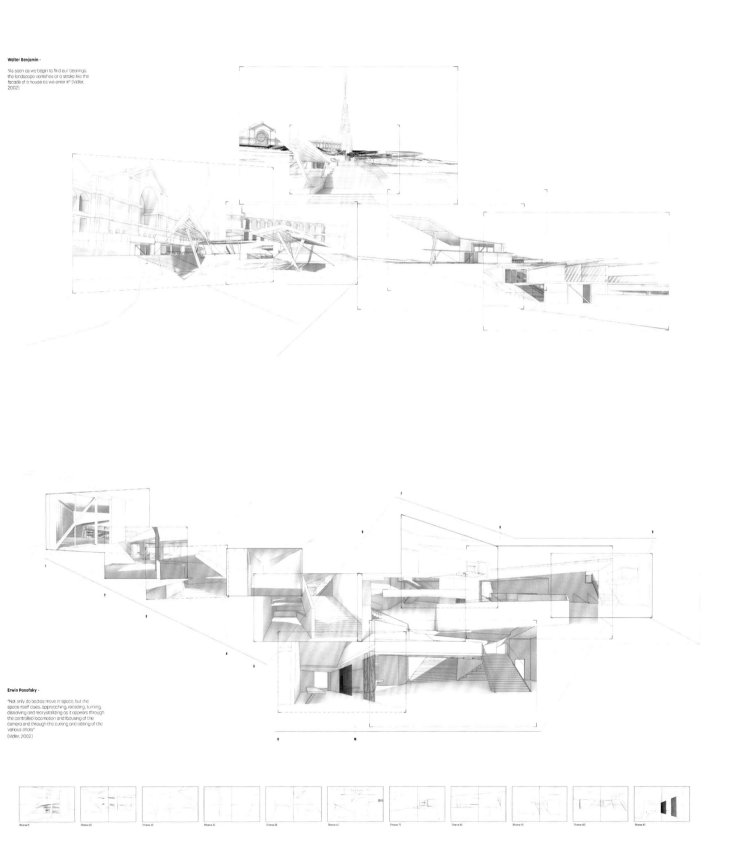

Walter Benjamin -

"As soon as we begin to find our bearings, the landscape vanishes at a stroke like the facade of a house as we enter it" (Vidler, 2002)

Erwin Panofsky -

"Not only do bodies move in space, but the space itself does, approaching, receding, turning, dissolving and recrystalizing as it appears through the controlled locomotion and focusing of the camera and through the cutting and editing of the various shots" (Vidler, 2002)

"The time is now ..."

Analogue Syntax
Perry Kulper

Title:
Architect, Associate Professor of Architecture, University of Michigan, Taubman College of Architecture + Urban Planning

Instagram:
@pkulper

Story

The development of a discipline for working, and teaching, has been provocative, intriguing and tangled. Fundamentally, my development has had to do with overcoming the crisis of reduction, or reducing things too quickly when working, and identifying the scope and fitness of a body of work, in particular situations. It has been motivated by augmenting typologies of representation with alternative ways to express ideas visually, best articulated as a movement towards working on things as structured relations, not necessarily as things, objects or figures; a movement from typological and conventional thinking to composites, hybrids and ecologies of marks; expanding visualisations from homogeneous aspects of drawing to the incorporation of multiple languages of representation (words, indexes, notational, unknowable relations, etc.); developing trust to utilise a full gradient, or range, of thinking positions that move between certainty and hunches.

The pleasurable challenges have been many: working on ideas, subjects or areas that weren't in the so-called canon, and don't lend themselves to immediate spatial enactment; temporally structured things; things that evade articulation, either conceptually or visually; convincing myself that alternative means of working are worthwhile.

FIND ME:

Inspiration

Each work, project or drawing starts differently, motivated by varied aspirations. It could be motivated by curiosity about a colour of acrylic pigment I have on my worktable, by researched and carefully framed ideas about a museum, or by interests in the spatial and representational potentials of erasure. The motivations might have to do with my growth, technique acquisition, nurturing my imagination, reframing former pieces of work, or cultural durability. It could be all those things, in the same project.

Often, when I start a drawing, I give it 'tasks' – a kind of programme, as it were. Importantly, the work varies from project to project, from phase to phase, and visualisations are tailored per the phase of work and the project being worked on. Some drawings describe a project, some discover things and others attempt to prove something.

Process

ANALOGUE SYNTAX

My drawings are specific to the phase of the work. While not always true in practice, ideally, each visualisation would be particular to what's being worked on, and when it's being worked on.
In my understanding, design methods are the ways we work on work. Representation techniques are the ways we work through design methods. I've identified 14 design methods. There are many more. I/We use them singularly, in combination and can even invent design methods. There are differing diagrams for the 'sequences' in which they might be utilised. Depending on what I am working on, I often use 'content to form' as a kind of meta method, in which other methods might be used. Common methods for me include appropriation, analogic thinking, metaphorical means and methods/techniques such as diagramming, notation and indexical means. Representation techniques include conventions, strategic plots, temporal choreographs, cryptic/genetic drawings, analogical visualisations and visualising critical fragments.
My interest in being versatile, dexterous and agile – that is being able to act differently, by a lot, in different situations – suggests trading on different design methods. By understanding highly varied and diverse design methods and representation techniques, you realise that some are more effective than others in particular situations. Advocating for multiple design methods, understanding their etymology, preferences/biases, ways in which authors interface with them, ways to operate with them and a repertoire of case studies, is critical to being able to act differently in different situations.

Tips

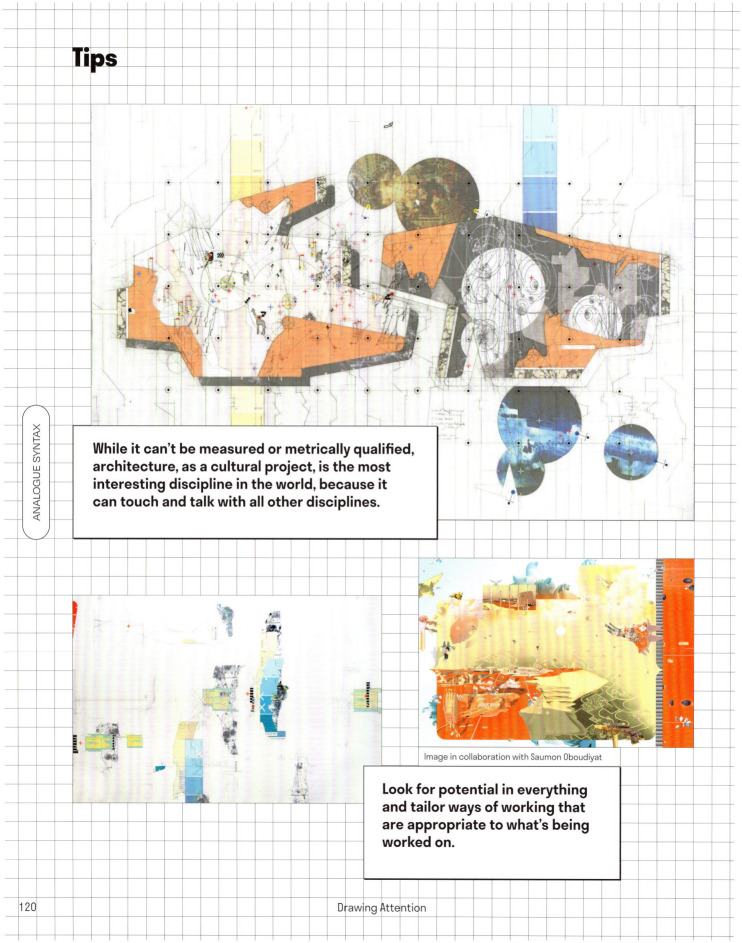

While it can't be measured or metrically qualified, architecture, as a cultural project, is the most interesting discipline in the world, because it can touch and talk with all other disciplines.

Image in collaboration with Saumon Oboudiyat

Look for potential in everything and tailor ways of working that are appropriate to what's being worked on.

> **Immerse yourself in looking at high-quality visual things: films, painting, sculpture and visualisations.**

Image in collaboration with Mark West

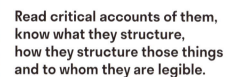

> **Read critical accounts of them, know what they structure, how they structure those things and to whom they are legible.**

Step by Step

The David's Island Ideas competition focused on a small island off the coast of New York. Historically, the island has been occupied by Siwanoy Indigenous Americans, various agricultural practices, a prospective ink factory, a military base and a regional power authority. Since 1973 there has been no sanctioned activity on the island, and the dominant military structures are now abandoned amid a regenerative natural environment.

The Strategic Plot oscillates between a concrete spatial proposal and notations for further development. It serves three primary purposes: to hold multiple languages of representation in play, simultaneously; to discover programmatic logics to 'carry' the content of the project; and to cultivate the drawing as a thing in and of itself. The spatial interventions are generated to augment, qualify and occasionally negate existing conditions – continually prompting the emergent temporal dynamics of the island.

The proposal for the island attempts productive engagement with a range of issues including, but not limited to: the islanders' experience of remoteness and isolation; the prevalence of maritime mythologies and folklore; the manifestations of divergent occupations; the cultural import of drift, migration and transience; the real and imagined sensing of suppressive panoramic and panoptic regimes; the representational practices of nautical cartography; the elusiveness of nocturnal ephemera; and the literal and strategic deployment of military jargon.

There are a number of interventions, including: landings for mythical sea travellers; axis of mutiny; camouflagic surfaces; landing 'vessel'; labyrinths of emptiness; mis-coordinated landscapes; machinic surveillance field; erosion surfaces; polished metamorphic rock gardens; 'ballasted' space; an attractive shell surface; 'easement' fencing; a 'multiplied' officer's headquarters; bird colony lines; photo 'ops'; panoramic steel walls and 'no fly zones' mingle with, interfere with and remain indifferent to the bounded and fugitive aspects of the island. Tactically disposed, these messengers tickle the history, physicality and projective aspects of the island and sea. New event infrastructures prompt a tensional play between tyrannies of control and borderless wandering, spawning a range of correspondences to limits and the unbounded.

Tools: Mylar, assorted found imagery, cut paper, foil, transfer letters, transfer film, tape, graphite, ink

1.

First, set up your workspace and drawing table. It is very important to prepare your workspace for hand drawings and collages. Clean and prep drawing instruments, templates, parallel rule, drawing surface and other gear. Make sure to prepare any referential material, and notes; this helps me set the agenda, or 'program' for drawing.

2.

Add rich tonal and textural grounds to use in the composition. Here, I print large copies of food images (photographed by Sophie Grigson). These pieces help to set up the 'programme' for the studies. Cut and apply the paper figures (seen in blue, yellow and grey), and try to build a stock of images, patterns and colours over time, to use for your ideas and drawings.

3.

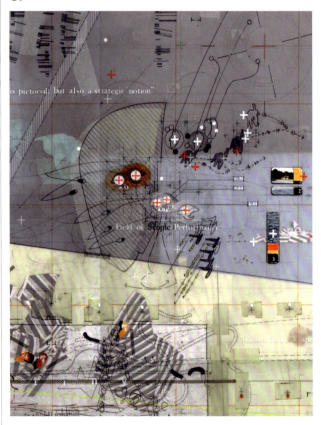

Using Mylar, a drawing film, begin to create layers and initial markings. Prepare 60 x 91 cm double matt Mylar and draw a kind of 'prototype' set of marks, to do with an ecology of 'players' in a relational field. Here, I explore temporal shifts, situated and extended geographic relations, and indeterminacy. Try to achieve these expressions using diagram-like marks and textual and symbolic notations.

4.

Continue to work on the composition in the 2D plane, as well as the 3D plane by layering on top of, and behind, the Mylar. Use drawn marks, cut paper collage, Letraset, tape, aluminium foil and animal X-rays. Indeterminacy can guide the work as you embrace hunches, certainties and flat-out shots in the dark, to discover the potential and scope of the drawing and spatial proposal.

5. [Overleaf]

Once the composition feels reasonably satiated, isolate the Mylar to reveal the line drawing. The spatial/architectural elements are separated from the landscape interventions, resulting in a first draft of the primary spatial elements, at particular scales. This shows the potential for multiple drawing outcomes when using serendipitous layering techniques.

"Skill is more important than talent; this is a good thing because skills can be learned."

Axonometric Scenes

s.y.h

Title:
Architect/Illustrator

Instagram:
@syh_design

Story

Aside from my illustrations, I am a practising architect, and studying the subject has had a huge influence on my illustration style, both in terms of drawing content and technique. The majority of my illustrations are isometric projections, although I didn't appreciate the versatility of the method until studying for my Master's degree. Initially I began drawing isometric illustrations in the standard diagrammatic format, but soon started exploring how linework variations, colours and lighting can turn a simple isometric into something much richer and more interesting.

Isometric illustrations are often used for diagrammatic or technical drawings, given their ability to clearly present three-dimensional objects. This is both a strength and a weakness; isometric drawings are incredibly clear and easy to understand, but tend to be clinical and lack a discernible atmosphere or mood. I try to subvert these qualities by adding atmosphere and character, while maintaining the visual clarity that makes the drawing style so distinctive. Isometric drawings also have no perspective; this means all imagery included on the canvas is presented equally, which aids an intricate, detailed drawing style.

FIND ME:

Inspiration

A recurrent theme within my work is it explores the way in which people interact with architecture at a human scale – generally in a playful, comic manner. The architecture tends to be exaggerated, representing either a real location or a mix of influences to create the fantastical. A lot of my work is based around how overwhelmingly large constructions are appropriated by humans.

Although having a strong concept can be a good starting point for a drawing, I would never let the lack of one stop me from putting pen to paper. You can be inspired by something mundane, and this is just as justified a reason as anything else. There's an authenticity in drawing something that's completely mundane and transforming it into something remarkable.

Process

My methodology in the early stages of an illustration is quite rigid, followed by experimentation in the later stages – exploring different colours, shading and overlays.

Although it's not necessary to have a rigid methodology, there are advantages to knowing exactly how you produced a piece of work. The techniques used can be incorporated again, and maybe even improved on to produce something new in the future.

Experimentation and varying your methodology usually means a feeling of uncertainty about the quality during the process. However, this is a good thing; it means you're not playing it safe and is an excellent way to improve your abilities. If you stick to the same methodology with every new illustration then you're unlikely to see a vast improvement in your work.

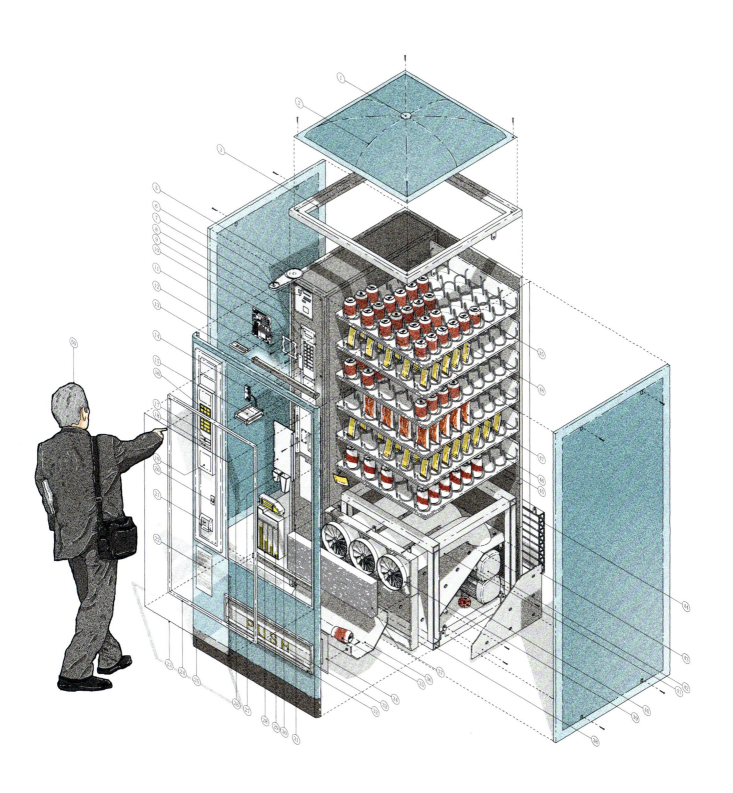

s.y.h

Tips

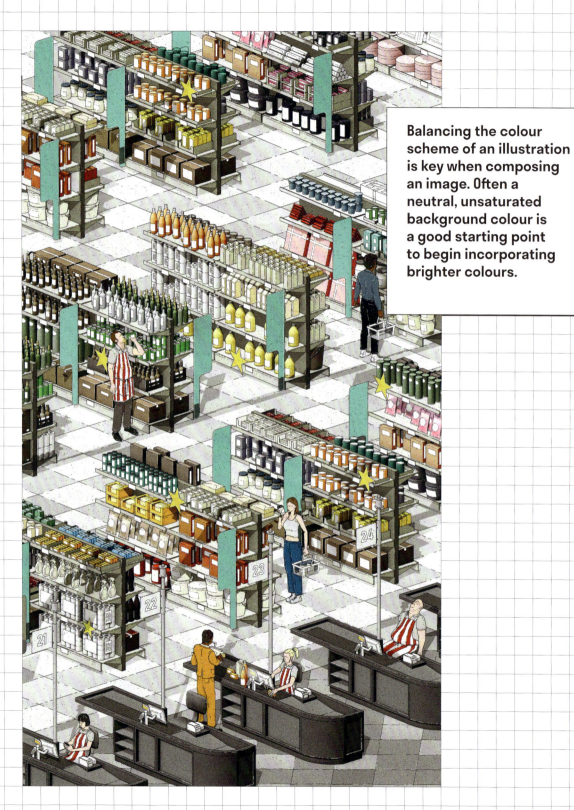

Balancing the colour scheme of an illustration is key when composing an image. Often a neutral, unsaturated background colour is a good starting point to begin incorporating brighter colours.

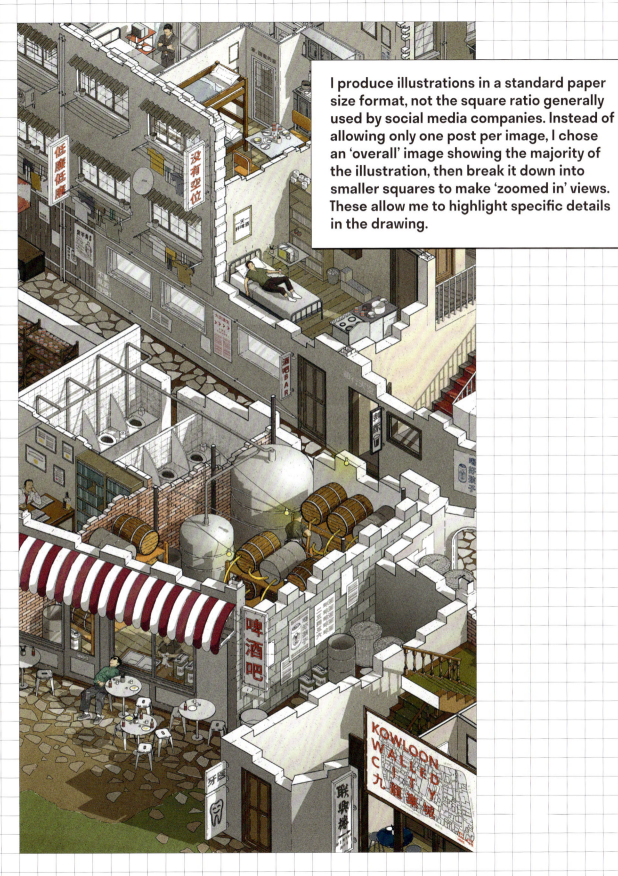

I produce illustrations in a standard paper size format, not the square ratio generally used by social media companies. Instead of allowing only one post per image, I chose an 'overall' image showing the majority of the illustration, then break it down into smaller squares to make 'zoomed in' views. These allow me to highlight specific details in the drawing.

Step by Step

I've always had an affection for Park Hill, the Brutalist residential block in Sheffield. However, it wasn't until I started my illustration that I could fully comprehend the complexity of the flats and the lengths to which the architects went to provide each flat with a front door on to the infamous 'streets in the sky'. Floor plans and sections do not do the flat layouts justice, and I learned a lot about the building, which has only furthered my admiration. I was interested in making a drawing that was clearly in a specific time period – the 1960s in this case. This was when the block was newly opened and the noble – or naive – ideas of the architects who designed it remained intact. This meant the colour schemes, the furniture, the outfits – the fact that everyone is smoking – together convey a distinct time, place and atmosphere.

Tools: Photoshop, Illustrator, Rhinoceros 3D, V-Ray

1.

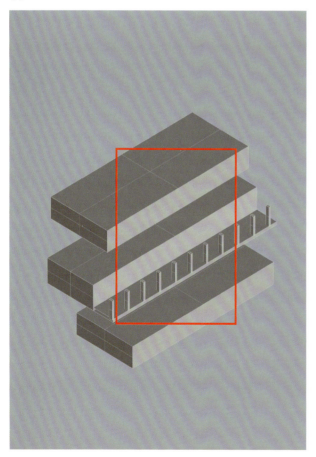

Start with a massing model to arrange the composition of the image. Include a frame outline of your intended canvas size (here highlighted red), so you know the exact boundaries of your drawing and won't waste time modelling things that aren't visible in the final image.

2.

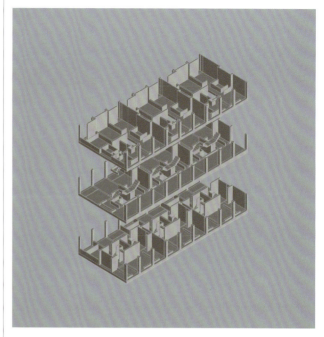

Add model detail such as brickwork and floor hatches. Utilise blocks/components so you never model the same thing twice. Further detail can be drawn later in Illustrator or **Photoshop**, especially organic form elements such as fabric or water.

3.

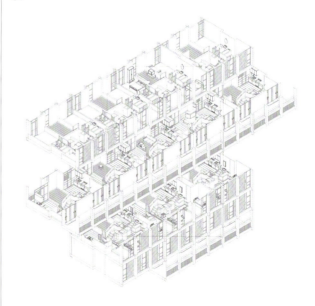

Export all linework as a PDF or DWG and a clay render of the model to add depth. These two elements will serve as the base layers of the final image. If you have illuminated elements, you'll have to render these separately with all other light sources switched off, in order to create the magic 'glowing' effect.

4.

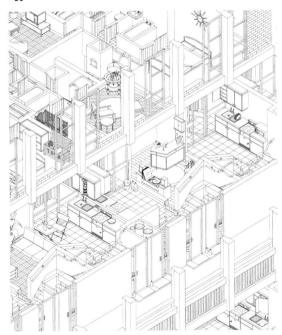

Open the PDF/DWG in Illustrator and initially change it to a uniform line weight. Vary the brush type to give the linework more variety and a less clinical, digital style.

5.

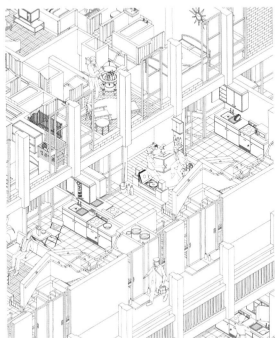

Draw in more details and figures. Drawing unique figures makes a huge impact on the overall quality of an illustration. You can use a digital stylus, but if you're struggling, find reference photos and trace them. If you've got a tight deadline, just use vectors off the internet instead.

6.

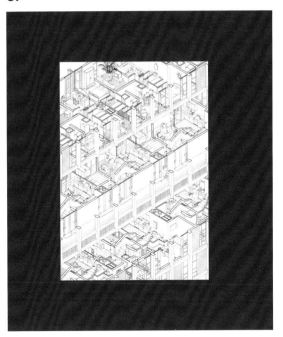

Varying the line thickness is an important step to add character and personality. The line weight depends on the canvas size, but at a minimum you need three different line weights. A thick line weight for the sectional cuts, a medium line weight for the majority of the drawing, and a thin line weight for any fine details. Export the vector linework as PNG files to import into **Photoshop**.

7.

Import all linework PNGs into **Photoshop**. Add all 3D renders from the model and place them behind the linework layers. Adjust the opacity of the renders to suit.

8.

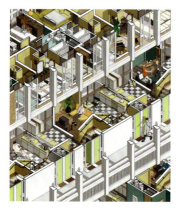

Fill most of the white space at an early stage. These base colours are likely to change as the drawing progresses, but the colouring process will seem less daunting once the page is full of colour.

9.

Add a grain overlay filter for subtle variations to the colours and linework. To create a grain filter, first create a new layer and fill it entirely with white. Then select Filter > Noise > Add Noise to create a grey 'white noise' effect. Change the layer to 'Overlay' and adjust opacity to suit.

10.

The balance between too dull and too colourful is a fine line, and it often comes down to trial and error. Keep experimenting and adjusting – you'll soon start to find the right balance.

11.

Add shiny reflections to any glass elements, and subtle highlights to brickwork and flooring. These extra touches are almost imperceptible to the viewer but add a richness and depth.

12.

Draw in line highlights to make elements in the illustration pop. These are semi-transparent white line highlights which sit along the edges of objects and figures. They're visible here on the television, stair tread and kitchen cabinets. Sit them behind the main linework layer at around 70% transparency. Adding dots can give additional texture on certain elements.

"It's not about how you draw. It's about what makes you pick up the pencil."

Digital Ink
Veronika Ikonnikova

Title:
**Illustrator and artist based in
Tokyo, architect at Kengo Kuma
and Associates**

Instagram:
@veronika_ikn

Story

Illustration is a way to explore and express the aesthetics of the
environment. My fascination with aesthetic environments began when
looking at architecture and interior design magazines we had in our home,
and later with the first trips to new places. I was particularly sensitive to
changes in natural conditions – light, air, rain or snow would create very
specific moods, as if each added an emotional layer to the environment.
Architectural studies at university provided me with a strong background
in traditional hand drawing and painting – mediums such as soft pencil,
pen and ink, and watercolour were my main tools at the time. However, I
have always loved digital art's ability to convey nuanced atmospherics –
for conveying the intricacies of such complex light conditions as floating
particles of dust in light rays, the ambient light of an overcast day, the
glow of artificial lights at night and so on. Motivated by those expressive
possibilities, I gradually taught myself digital painting and illustration.

FIND ME:

Inspiration

Most of my inspiration comes from my immediate surroundings, which is why the beauty and harmony of the environment around me is important. I came to Tokyo five years ago with a strong appreciation of Japanese environmental aesthetics – first and foremost in order to immerse myself in them, and to learn from this place firsthand. As this city has become my home, my understanding has deepened, and my curiosity has only increased. My illustrations carry a persistent and personal sensibility of my Japanese environment.

Process

I suggest consciously separating two modes of work: creative and critical. When in creative mode, allow yourself to sketch and jot down ideas freely, and stop yourself from judging them at this point. It is best if you can allow ample time for this stage, since it is difficult to go into this mode under the pressure of deadlines. After you have recorded many ideas and given yourself a break in the process, return to them in critical mode: look at the ideas as though they were someone else's. That is, look at them objectively as much as possible. Select the most promising ones and keep developing those, alternating between the creative and critical modes of work.

Tips

When travelling, notice and record (sketch, write, photograph) interesting aspects of the environment. This will be useful when you draw an imaginary building or a setting. For the imaginary bamboo treehouse I draw inspiration from the stilt structure of Kiyomizu Dera in Kyoto, and the roof is a typical clay roof often found in traditional residential and temple architecture in Japan.

In order to achieve special lighting effects –
like a strong reflection of sunset light from
a glass facade – experiment with blending
modes. A warm colour with a soft round brush
in 'Color Dodge' mode is excellent for highlights.
However, there is no single recipe for all
occasions – experiment with the blending
modes and colors, to see what works for
each particular illustration.

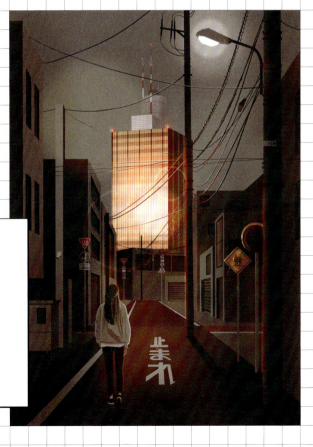

A good exercise in understanding light is to
take an existing place as a base, and paint
it in an imaginary light condition. This how
this illustration was done. The shrine is based
on a real one in Tokyo; however, the lighting
scenario is made up. Once you understand
lighting basics, you can render any lighting
scenario you can imagine.

Step by Step

Tectonics of Time is largely the culmination of what I experienced and learned in five years of living in Japan. Most of the architecture here is made up, but the modern towers reference Tokyo, while the traditional architecture is reminiscent of Nara and Kyoto.

Part of the idea is based on my Master's thesis research done in the University of Tokyo titled 'Rooftop Urbanism',[6] in which I documented various usages of rooftop spaces currently present in the city, and discussed the potential of using currently unoccupied rooftop space.

For this drawing, I explore a fictional but reality-grounded scenario of future Tokyo. As the population density and land prices are ever-increasing, more and more people move to the rooftops of larger buildings – rising above countless offices and dwellings, they gain a bit more autonomy, while remaining closely linked to the central areas. The density of the underlying city fabric makes it possible to connect some of the nearby rooftops into a continuous walkway, or a street. In the vastness of the rooftop level, some people start recreating the old townscapes of Tokyo from different eras (Edo, Meiji). Removed from the bustle of the city traffic and in the quiet and peace of the city's rooftops, one can experience the spirituality and magic of old Japan in the heart of the metropolis.

Tools: Wacom Cintiq, Photoshop

1.

Spend extra time on initial sketches – keep them small (thumbnails) and make many. Use annotations to record key aspects next to them. The more time you spend on initial sketches, the more solid your base will be, and the more successful the result.

2.

Once happy with the sketch, set it to 'Multiply' blending mode (in **Photoshop** – here and onwards) with a bit of transparency, and start blocking out main volumes in perspective. Use single-colour flat shading for the building volumes – this is helpful for quick selection (via the Magic Wand tool or the 'Select' menu – 'Color Range') and allows for easy compositional/perspective adjustment at this stage.

3.

With the rooftop structures as the main focus, sketch them in more detail, referring to the more precise building volumes.

4.

Paint some of the foreground focus elements in greater detail. Since this is digital illustration, the order of painting (background/foreground) is less important.

5.

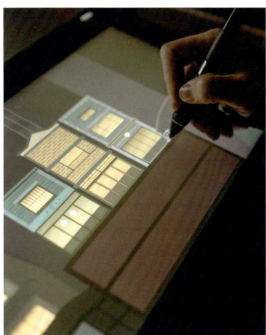

After the foreground, the second focus area is the middle ground. It is a continuous street formed by multiple connected buildings. As it develops, think up new details – the particular design of buildings and the structure that is supporting them.

6.

Keep developing the image by adding more detail (here – buildings, street lights, electric poles). To indicate glow, for instance streetlights and highlights on the wires, use a soft-edge brush in 'Color Dodge' blending mode. Make sure your 'Pressure for Opacity' is on – this is excellent for light glow effects.

7.

Alternate freely between different areas of the canvas as you keep adding detail – this helps keep the composition balanced.

8.

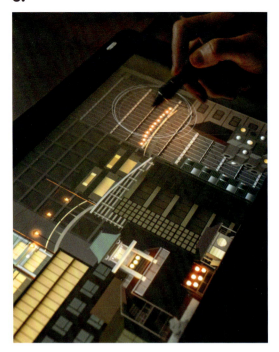

By adding window lights, and direct and reflected light from light poles on the buildings around, the image is turned from flat blocks into a visually coherent environment.

9.

In the final stages, refine the overall exposure by making the whole image a bit darker and emphasising the light glow of the old structures. Adjustment layers such as 'Exposure' or 'Curves' combined with layer masks provide a lot of flexibility.

10.

To suggest 'life' and some narrative, keep adding detail – silhouettes, lights in the storefronts, streetlights and street elements, etc. This step can be applied only to the focus areas, or to the image as a whole.

Line Ideation
Fraser Morrison

Title:
**Master's tutor at TU Eindhoven,
designer at Architecture 00,
co-founder of Future // Fields
and Flere Atelier**

Instagram:
@fraser_momo

Often, we use complex imagery to convey the lengths we have gone to in a project. After all, the labour can feel meaningless if not represented in its fullest form. But often, the complexity can lay bare the unresolved aspects of your project. In pursuit of a dynamic and complex graphical and architectural response, these drawings can conceal the original intention and conceptual clarity.

Paring your imagery back can aid you in resolving more difficult areas of your design. To apply this process, ask yourself three questions: What you are saying with the drawing? What needs to be emphasised? What medium is best to illustrate the idea? What the drawing says is paramount. Writing a small sentence or 'headline' at the start of the project forces you to distil the essence of your proposal into a few words. If the sentence doesn't capture the heart of your design, a portfolio filled with text will not provide more understanding. For instance, if your project site is in a mountainous area, your design could be responding to this complex site and outstanding beauty. How does your design address the site? Which spatial arrangement is important to you? How does it open out to the view? What are you responding to in your design?

Present a hierarchy of information. Establishing what to highlight and what is background information aids both the legibility of your idea and clarity in your thinking. The element in your drawing that requires most emphasis can sometimes be captured by a philosophical or technical question.

FIND ME:

Ask yourself these questions when drawing: Which tools are you going to use? Is a sketch enough? Could a digital line drawing be the most evocative? What details need to be softened? Where are the large gestures?

Varying line weights can be all you need to express a narrative. Consider the use of only three line weights, you can split the information into categories: wide, thin and fine.

- Thin lines form the background of the drawing, best understood as the 'bones' of the image that give it a legible spatial configuration.
- Wide lines catch the eye and should generally be used to highlight the focal point of your project by outlining specific elements, which brings forward the form against the backdrop of finer elements.
- Fine lines provide other details, whether the materiality of a wall, or foliage and other forms of animation. Control of these adds texture, while making more complex information form part of the background instead of detracting from the overall composition.

The medium is equally fundamental to your project's success. *Digital drawings* that combine visual information and axonometric drawing can create a clear and balanced image. *Axonometric drawing* takes a variety of forms and is driven by the angle at which a space is projected.

Each of the questions above asks you to take a minute and question your position and your ideas. Taking the time to be critical of your work and to be able to understand which things need to be discussed more or less is vital to your future in the profession.

Clarity of visual representation will aid your verbal communication, among other things. Stripping back complex drawings can help strengthen your argument, as each illustration should be able to stand alone without you there to explain it. Simplifying your architectural drawings doesn't mean that you have thought about your project less, but rather that you have been self-critical and thought about it more.

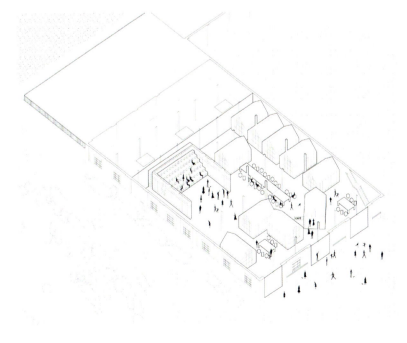

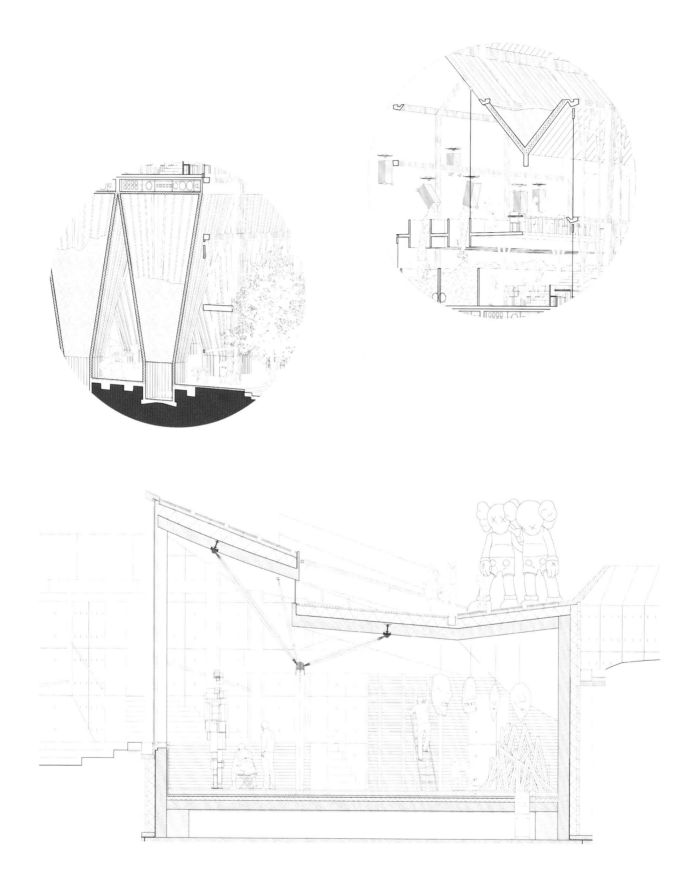

Drawing Attention

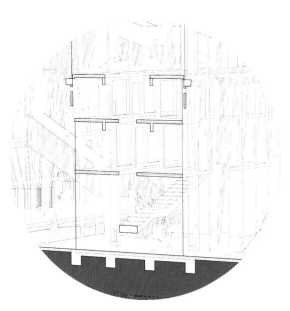

"All great designs started with a line!"

The Procreative
Ehab Alhariri

Title:
**Principal architect at
4Space Design**

Instagram:
@archihab

Story

While working as an architect over the years, a notepad has always been at my desk for sketching whatever comes to mind. Whether related to a project or not, it's helped to improve my sketching skills as I am constantly practising and recording my ideas. I would use these ideas later and develop them into full projects to share with my followers online. Some of these projects went viral and were featured in several architectural outlets. I would advise all architects to keep a record of their ideas because it can lead to greater things down the line.

FIND ME:

Inspiration

Although having a strong concept is crucial when designing a project, it's something I care less about when sketching or making an illustration. While I am bound by several constraints when designing for a project, I find myself free and liberated when sketching and making illustrations for my Instagram page. It opened doors for me to explore and experiment with new ideas, improving my design skills and eye for detail. The concept is important, but the main factor for sketching is to improvise and let loose. Letting your hand and imagination go is where the magic happens, and simple ideas can be refined into concepts.

Process

It usually starts with a fast sketch on my sketching pad. Later, I take a picture and use it as a reference for my illustration. Here is where I change the medium to digital, as it gives me a lot of control over my drawing, especially with the layers, brushes and textures I can create. For that, I use an iPad with the Apple Pencil and **Procreate**. Using this device and app allows me the most flexibility, as I find the pen pressure and angle over the screen resemble a real pen and paper. In my opinion, **Procreate** has the best balance between artistic and architectural features compared to other applications.

Tips

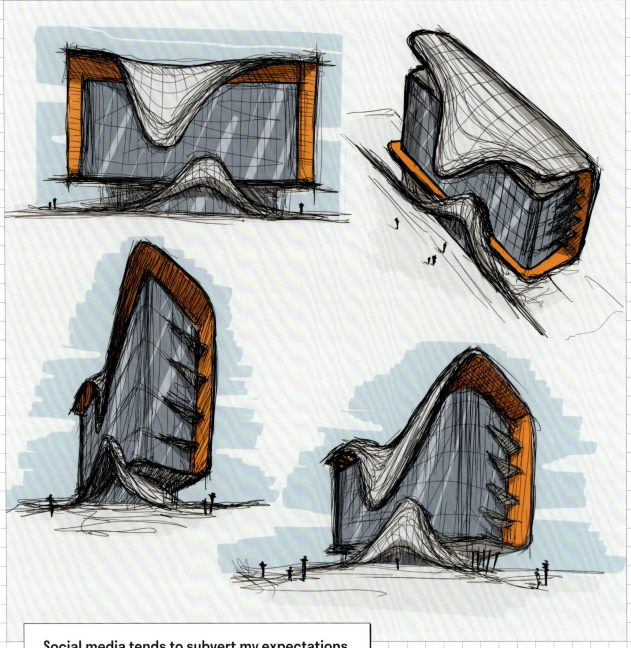

Social media tends to subvert my expectations.
I expect certain illustrations to go viral, but
the ones I don't usually draw attention.

How do you go viral on social media? The best way is by providing value for users, whether in the form of knowledge, entertainment or creative approaches.

Adding simple concept diagrams to an illustration adds a lot of value and makes it more likely to be liked.

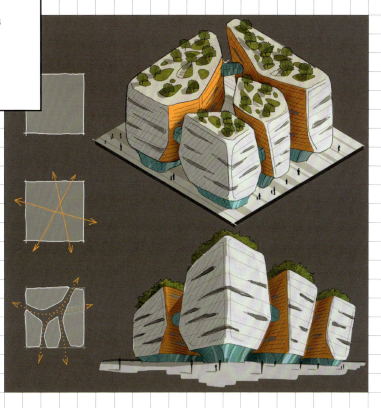

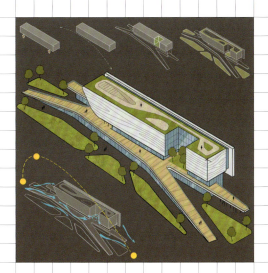

Step by Step

For this illustration, I want to create a futuristic design with a robotic-looking box-shaped building that has a mysterious function we can't yet comprehend. This is my favourite type, which I rarely get the chance to draw for a few reasons. First, it is time-consuming and difficult due to the details required to achieve the desired look. Second, it's not always popular with social media algorithms and can fall short on engagement compared to other types. Sometimes, you feel obliged to do what you think will be successful and ignore what you actually want to create, but I try to find a balance between what the algorithm wants me to do and what I want to do. It gives me the drive to continue creating content online.

Tools: Apple iPad, Apple Pencil, Procreate, Lightroom

1.

Start with a hand sketch in a sketching pad, which gives you freedom to explore different ideas. After scanning, this sketch became the base.

2.

Take a picture or scan your hand sketch, then import it into your drawing app, using an **iPad**, **Apple Pencil** and **Procreate**. Trace over the hand sketch, adding details to make it clearer for the final inking stage. This step can be repeated as much as necessary by adding a new layer and drawing over the old one until the sketch feels right.

3.

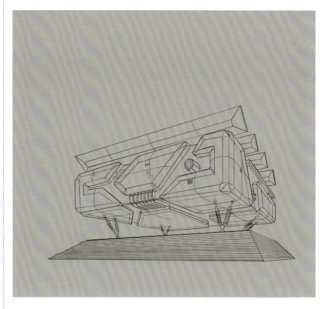

Now the rough sketch is ready, create a new layer for 'clean lines'. Try the **Procreate** perspective grid by assigning the vanishing points that correspond with the rough sketch points. The technical pen brush is well suited to this task and helps to make a more accurate illustration.

4.

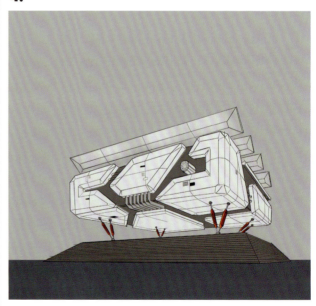

Fill the clean lines layer with the basic colours, by dropping the chosen colour inside a region. It's better to put the base colour on a different layer from the clean lines layer, as this gives you control over the effects and textures needed to add to the colours later. You can set the clean lines layer as 'Reference'.

5.

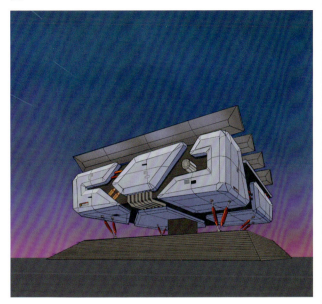

Put in a background to assess the ambience of the illustration, then add the shadows and highlight accordingly. Draw the shadows and highlights as black and white in a new layer, then reduce the transparency to 35% to 50%, depending on the desired contrast. For the ambience, mask the building with a colour close to the background colour, then change its settings to 'Overlay' to help the building fit into the environment.

6.

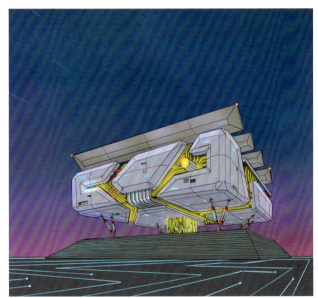

Add the lights and details to the building to give it a futuristic sci-fi look. For the light effect, try 'Light Pen' for the lines or use the 'Add layer' settings for large regions.

7.

To complete the illustration, we need a sense of the surroundings – here, a futuristic city skyline. It can be hard to come up with designs from your imagination, so it's always a good idea to look for refences from existing or other imaginary projects. As example, one of the towers in the background was inspired by Zaha's Hadid Dancing towers project. Consider including human figures to add a sense of scale and tell a story.

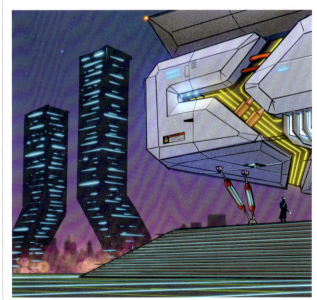

8.

The last step is to transfer the drawing to your computer for final colour correction using Lightroom or **Photoshop**. In this way you can add contrast and saturation to make the colours less flat.

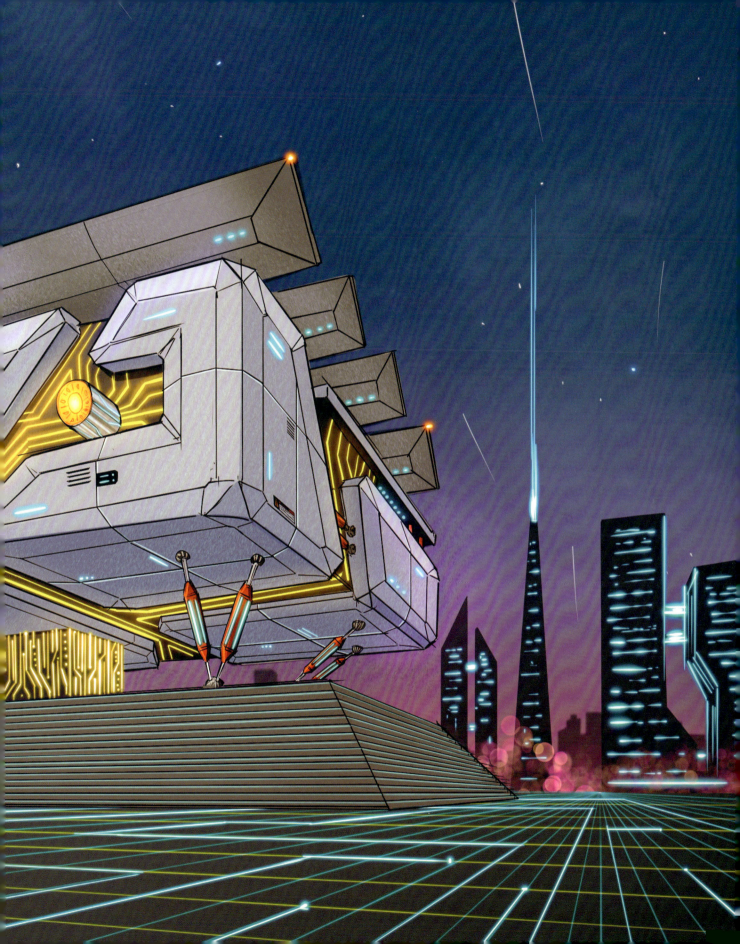

"The drawing is a space of wonder, waiting to be inhabited."

Pencil and Eraser
Clement Luk Laurencio

Title:
Architectural designer, artist

Instagram:
@clementluklaurencio

Story

I've always drawn, but was never any good at depicting people. Instead, I took to landscapes and buildings, which naturally pushed me towards architecture. Hand-drawing skills have developed throughout my architectural education, though it took time to build confidence. I remember creating computer renderings for my final project in third year, but they didn't truly capture the essence and atmosphere of what I had in my head. The only way I could get that across was by doing it by hand, and from then on, I could never abandon hand drawing. Lebbeus Woods' drawings hold a special place in my heart. It was only after coming across his incredible draughtsmanship that I saw the possibilities of drawing … the longer you look, the more you discover; the more you discover, the deeper you delve into his architectural worlds. It's what I strive for: to create a world on paper where the viewer can immerse themselves and momentarily escape in a daydream.

FIND ME:

Inspiration

Recent drawings have been inspired by questions, rather than concepts: 'If I were to draw all of the spatial memories I could recall, what would that look like?' or 'What spaces would emerge if I created a drawing which combined Jorge Luis Borges' two fictions into one drawing?' Starting from a question means you can approach the drawing as an act of exploration and discovery, rather than a way to simply represent.

Following background research based on the theme of the question, I look at other drawings, watch films, observe art or photography, or read novels or texts which also deal with what I am exploring. Understanding the subject on a deeper level provides more inspiration, and knowing what has been done already opens new avenues and perspectives. Whichever way you begin a drawing – from a question, a concept or anything else – a strong interest and curiosity will push you to greater heights!

Process

While researching, I take notes and make small rough sketches in my notebook using a pen to capture my intuitive thoughts about composition, elements, spatial explorations and other ideas. After that, I begin to put pencil to paper. Using graphite can be a long process, but it offers time to think even while drawing. Every now and then, I stop and take a step back. It's important to see the whole picture, and to think critically about the drawing. If it's missing something, I go back to researching, or if I'm uninspired, I begin work on another piece. Coming back to it after time helps me tackle the drawing feeling refreshed and reinvigorated. Everyone develops their own methodology over time, and it happens intuitively. The more I draw, the more I learn about myself and the processes I go through to create a drawing, and I'm sure you will too.

Tips

Step back from your drawing. By observing your work from afar, you may find new meaning and spatial relationships which you had yet to consider. If you feel stuck, leave your drawing to 'simmer' by taking a break.

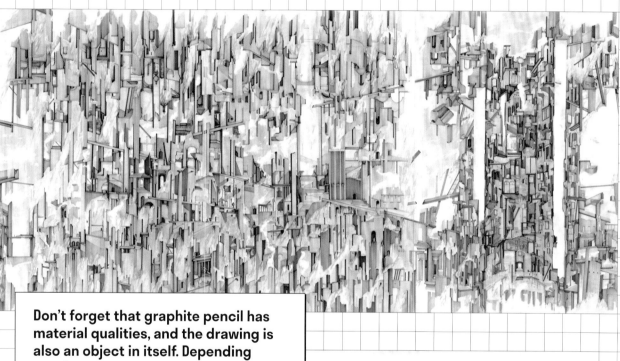

Don't forget that graphite pencil has material qualities, and the drawing is also an object in itself. Depending on where one stands, the darkest shade can obscure forms and spaces, while the slightest shift can reflect the light. Consider how the viewer might move around your drawing.

Drawing by hand forces you to confront the size of the drawing in relation to your own body. Whether you are making a quick sketch on site, or a scale drawing, the direct link between the pencil, your hand and the line gives you a more intimate understanding of the space you're drawing.

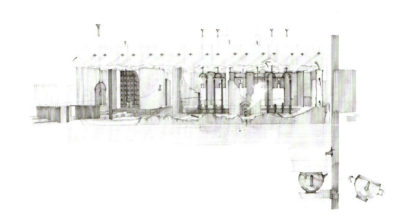

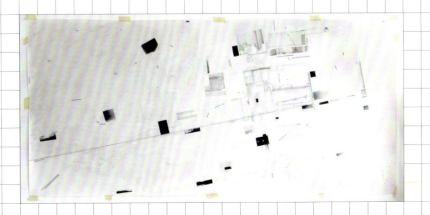

Clement Luk Laurencio

Step by Step

'Pavilions for Conversations, View towards the Thames' was one of the final drawings made for my fourth-year Master's project. It was done under the end-of-year time constraints, which students will be familiar with.

Description of the project: 'In light of the New Silk Road linking China to the UK, this project explores the notion of the tea ceremony as an act of conversation and cooperation between countries. Traces of movements have been recorded on a tablecloth from an experimental tea ceremony ritual. From these movements, the pavilions were designed and created. The architecture is elemental in nature, with the pavilions acting as sheltering stone caverns, providing a place for conversations to flourish and disputes to be settled.

Designed to survive the future rise in global sea levels, the Pavilions are to become lasting landmarks, approachable by boat. The sandstone roofs will be filtering the rainwater to be used for the tea ceremony, for generations to come.'

Tools: Hand drawing, graphite pencil

PENCIL AND ERASER

1.

Gather your drawing tools. Use pencils of varying softness for tones and shades, mechanical pencils for detail work, soft and hard erasers, and rulers or circle templates. In terms of softness/hardness of the graphite, anything from 2H to 4B will help you achieve a dynamic range of shades.

2.

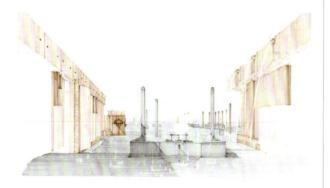

Set the scene and carefully consider the composition of your drawing. Situating the view will not only contextualise the building but will also draw the viewer towards your image. Find a viewpoint which makes it feel as if the viewer were standing within your proposal; keep in mind the eye level and horizon line.

3.

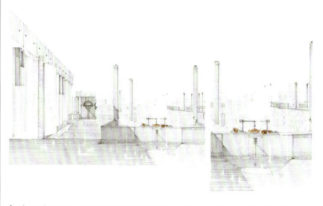

Scale and space – people are important to understand the scale of buildings, and objects such as teapots, handrails or steps can have a similar function.

4.

Tonal range – start off light with a 2H pencil and work your way up in softness to create more contrast. It is difficult to say when to use an HB or a 4B, but over time, you will find the contrast and techniques that work for you and your drawing.

5.

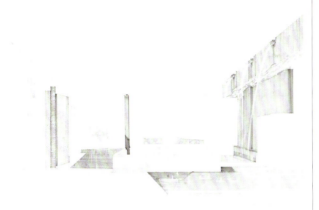

Textures and mass – spend time adding the necessary details to the objects, surfaces and structures within your scene. This will influence how your scene 'feels': is the surface of the stone smooth, so I can imagine running my hand across it? Does it reflect the light, so it illuminates part of the composition? Does it look heavy, so it holds a strong architectural presence? Looking closely at the stone roof, the smooth surfaces contrast with the rough edges that have been chipped off over time.

6.

Don't forget that erasing is also a form of mark-making and drawing. You can erase areas to highlight them. These are meant to be subtle and ephemeral touches, which draw the viewer closer.

7.

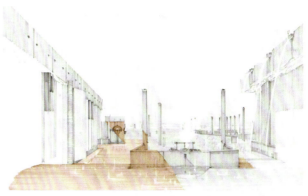

Without shadow, the scene doesn't have that quality which anchors it to reality. Adding this to your drawing will not only help give depth to your space, but will also set the atmosphere of the drawing.

8.

Architecture is fundamentally an experience. Since student work remains unbuilt, we have no choice but to communicate this intangible feeling through the language of drawing. Heavy rain is an evocative natural setting, which any viewer can 'hear' in their heads.

9.

Finally, the narrative is what will give life to your spaces. Leave signs of dwelling, as this will keep the viewer wondering what the story behind them is. Here, clouds of steam hint that someone was just here and left in a hurry, also suggesting that the viewer is not alone in this space: intrigue and mystery are powerful elements in storytelling.

Avinet Laron
2019 M

"You can use drawing to explore, create and portray your own identity."

Art is Artefact
Zain Al-Sharaf Wahbeh

Title:
**Part II architecture student
at the Royal College of Art**

Instagram:
@designs.by.zain

Story

Born in Jordan and raised in the United Arab Emirates, I am a Palestinian academic and designer who has immersed herself in architectural practice for the past six years.

It has become a colossal responsibility for me to establish unique methods of digital storytelling and forensic archival mapping. This was driven by urgency to digitally reconstruct and preserve vernacular design aspects of my no-longer-existing Palestinian hometown. I found that the most effective way to address the challenges of inventing novel methods of archiving and cultural reconstruction is to experiment with various perspectives and drawing styles. This exploration involved referring to the works of architects and illustrators who have successfully implemented narrative-driven drawings, such as Paul Noble, Alexander Brodsky and Cinta Vidal.

FIND ME:

Inspiration

To any illustrator struggling with generating concepts for drawings: delve deeper into causes that most closely appeal to your upbringing, social encounters and heritage. Consider your agency as a designer in addressing your sites' most imperative socioeconomic, environmental and cultural challenges through critical design thinking and drawing. Ask yourself: how can your drawings be utilised to convey principles of inclusivity, social sustainability and structural integrity? Correspondingly, what type of details should be prioritised to convey the ethos of your design decisions? I approach my vocation as an agent of social justice and cultural preservation. Deploying a myriad of forensic, journalistic and illustrative practices that empower marginalised voices has arguably become my most fulfilling duty as a Palestinian researcher and designer. I strongly believe that the tenacity needed to digitally immortalise and relive aspects of my heritage is the driving force behind my most recent collection of drawings.

Process

Before beginning any type of illustration, render or a combination of the two, I produce numerous sketches and blueprints in various perspectives and scales. These tools help me determine the requirements and challenges that accompany each drawing. In the case of architecture, producing these drawings boils down to selecting the appropriate scale, perspective, colour scheme, linework and level of detail. These preliminary considerations help determine what style of drawing is most appropriate to communicate the most important aspects of the design, as well as save time during the process.

While I normally opt for sectional axonometric drawings, I have recently taken an interest in portraying cultural narratives through perspective elevation renders. By zooming in on street-level interactions in vernacular Palestine, these types of representations demand a skilled attention to detail, as well as consolidating multiple cultural elements in a single drawing. With that said, while it is important to keep an open mind when testing out various styles and compositions, it is also crucial to plan the requirements of your drawings beforehand. This will not only save you time, but will also keep you focused on the central criteria throughout the process.

Tips

Exploded sectional perspectives can be instrumental in explaining a building's structural, functional and stylistic makeup.

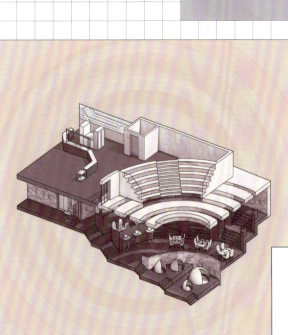

Details matter. You can express character and context through facade expression and displaying everyday 'life objects'.

To produce images with powerful narratives, layer your 3D model with relevant objects and textures that capture the essence of the designs, sites and time periods represented.

Fade out the rendered layer underneath the vector linework to create a realistic illustration look.

Step by Step

Traversing the reimagined Palestinian neighbourhood

Home to my paternal great grandparents, Al-Manshiyya was a Palestinian neighbourhood in the north of Jaffa. It faced a series of paramilitary attacks and mass demolitions under a brutal Zionist colonial occupation between 1948 and the present day. To confront the erasures of Al-Manshiyya's architecture, land and culture, I have initiated a restorative cultural practice that forensically examines and reconstructs the most crucial vernacular aspects of this now-absent neighbourhood. Titled 'The Image as an Archive', this project achieves reconstructions by drawing references from an extensive range of archival data. This includes but is not limited to scarce photographs of the neighbourhood and personal testimonies of Palestinian exiles gathered from interviews and schematic drawings.

Grounded in street-level interactions, the following illustration depicts typical Arabo-Islamic design archetypes such as window grilles and traditional shopfronts, as well as domestic furniture that was characteristic of Arab Palestine before the 1948 Nakba (exodus). It charts an alternative territory, by framing the most up-close-and-personal rudiments of a once-thriving Palestinian neighbourhood. In doing so, 'The Image as an Archive' aims to address my hometown's destruction, by enabling its audience to experience its past through contemporary modes of visualisation. A fundamental aspect of generating a powerful, narrative-driven drawing is including components that are authentic to the site and time period. In this case, I surveyed reference images of vernacular Palestinian buildings in Jaffa before 1948, and scrutinised details of objects and textures that were commonplace in domestic and commercial spaces. This exercise proved instrumental to reconstructing a vernacular essence with clarity and historical accuracy. I am indebted to my primary interviewee, Dr Ahmad Sharkas, for his extensive testimonies and for allowing me to interpret memories of his childhood home in this drawing. I couldn't have achieved an accurate representation of a generic Palestinian vernacular dwelling in Al-Manshiyya without his input.

Tools: Rhino 3D, Lumion 10, Photoshop, AutoCAD, Illustrator

1.

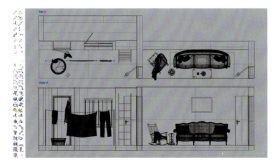

Software used: Rhino 3D
Produce a consolidated 3D model using original and imported components. Feel free to browse Quixel Megascans, Sketchfab and **SketchUp** 3D Warehouse for additional modelling assets that can enrich your illustration with more context. The more detail you can incorporate into the digital model, the more powerful the composition and narrative will be.

2.

Software used: Rhino 3D
Ensure that each modelled component is carefully categorised based on the material that it will be assigned. Use as many layers as necessary to establish these distinctions with different materials. Once completed, export the 3D model as a DWG file.

3.

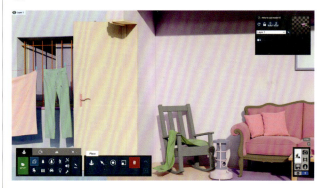

Software used: Lumion 10
Import the DWG file into the Lumion 10 rendering engine. On doing so, you will find that the model's layers can be easily identified and subsequently modified.

4.

Software used: Lumion 10
Take some time to determine the most appropriate camera angle for the final render. Adjust the perspective, camera height and focal lengths accordingly.

5.

Software used: Lumion 10
Assign the appropriate materials to each layer of components. Adjust the colourisation, reflectivity, relief and scale of each texture with consideration. To achieve a weathered or eroded appearance, use the weathering panel to adjust the extent of that effect. You can import your own textures or use the existing options in the software's materials library.

6.

Software used: Lumion 10
To create a long drawing, it is recommended that you horizontally divide the scene into two or more segments. These can be pieced together in post-production editing. Use the left and right arrows to define the extents of each scene.

7.

Software used: Lumion 10
Export the render in a high-quality 'Print' or 'Poster' setting. Be sure to save the material ID map for the post-production editing stage.

8.

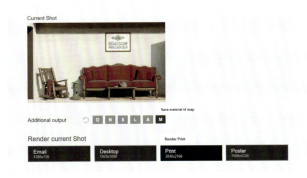

Software used: Photoshop
Connect the rendered segments with one another in **Photoshop**. Modify the elements of the scene wherever necessary. Use the material ID map to select individual components more easily. It will also be useful to label and group all the **Photoshop** layers in a clear and organised manner.

9.

Software used: AutoCAD and Illustrator
To establish a subtle illustration effect, trace the most important details of the rendered image. Be sure to assign different layers and colours to define varying line colours and thicknesses.

10.

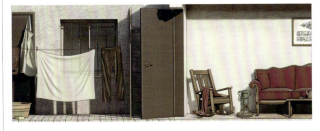

Software used: Illustrator
Reduce the opacity of the rendered image to 90–95%. Then format all the line categories in the drawing with their appropriate colours, opacities and line weights. After completing this stage, group all the lines together and reduce the linework layer's opacity to 65–70%.

ART IS ARTEFACT

Zain Al-Sharaf Wahbeh

Observational Sketch
Hammad Haider

Title:
Architectural assistant at HLM Architects, MArch Collaborative Practice at SSoA, Aziz Foundation Scholar, urban sketcher and calligrapher

Instagram:
@ink.sketcher

Hand drawing is a fundamental tool for architectural communication. The raw touch of pencil on paper draws out a certain magic that can't be showcased through any other means.

This practice of urban sketching is widely used, and everyone has their own approach; some combine ink with watercolour while others utilise a purely monochrome palette. The drawing could be of a landmark in the city or a scene in which a certain activity is taking place. To further enhance that drawn dialogue, I would also in that process take a photograph of the sketch with the scene itself to provide an almost direct reference between the drawing and the moment (as shown in the examples). This slowly developed into a creative portfolio, which I take pride in sharing. At present I can't go anywhere without taking my sketchbooks and pens with me. I believe that this sort of spontaneity in drawing without any restraints allows you to really immerse yourself in that moment and gives the drawing quite a unique energy; the life in that scene translates into the strokes that are being made. While drawing live you combine what you see, feel and hear into an arrangement of lines that aims to represent that narrative. As a professional in the architectural domain, you begin to also deconstruct that which is taking place around you and reconstruct it once again through your own lens.

Hand drawing allows you to illustrate design thoughts and processes which often aren't perfect, or complete illustrations in comparison to digitally created images which predominantly show a finished result. It is greatly beneficial to have conversations with your tutor with sketches to hand, and these can be overlaid with further developments

FIND ME:

with elements in other colours. To be able to use digital tools as well as hand drawing is truly beneficial in creating work with a hybrid quality. In a way it's a very engaging exercise, and adopting this approach very early on allows you to be able to utilise such tools later in professional practice.

Urban sketching as a component of site analysis

The concept of placemaking is central in ensuring a successful design scheme, and actively engaging and responding to the site context is paramount.

When it comes to initially analysing the site and its character, drawing from observation provides an interesting starting point for a project. Capturing the activity and the apparent opportunities/constraints through a visual map gives you a headstart in that crucial concept stage. As a student with a sketchbook, drawing out the architectural promenade and illustrating the views in and out of the site immerses you in that form-finding process.

The following are some general tips from a fellow urban sketcher:

1. Invest in a pocket-size or A5 sketchbook that is easy to carry.
2. Carry certain stationery that fits your drawing style – that could just be tones of monochrome pencil, a set of fineliners or even a string of primary-colour pencils or a mini watercolour box. Each one of these adds a certain quality and depth to the sketch.
3. Find a spot in which you can comfortably sit or stand and observe the scene.
4. Start by briefly setting out the page and gauge the proportions very loosely with a few pencil strokes.
5. Proceed to the main body of the sketch with varying strokes and line weights. This can be made easier with pen sets that have a range of tip thicknesses.
6. Don't worry about being accurate; aim to capture the main points of activity or features. Urban sketching has a free style and doesn't have any formal rules.
7. Capture your sketch and the process in location with your mobile device or a camera.
8. Sketch as a group or with your friends and become part of online urban sketching groups through social media. Gather inspiration and join the sketching community.

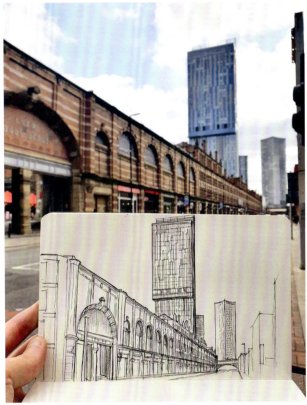

"There are no mistakes – it's all an experiment ..."

Drawing Attention

Ghibli Effect
Karina Armanda

Title:
**Architectural designer
and illustrator**

Instagram:
@karinaarmanda

Story

I was always fascinated with different styles of presentation and decoration. Back in primary school, when everyone had to bring a handmade card for some celebration, I created the 3D design using different parts of a mechanical watch which I found in my dad's toolbox. This fascination has never faded, even years later at architecture school. Every semester I have experimented with different styles – coloured pencil drawings, collages or a mix of both. The results were not always satisfying, but at least I tried. Photorealistic renders always ended up with me adding so many Photoshop layers you could barely see the initial render. I quickly gave up on software-generated images and pursued alternative ways of visualisation. The highlight of this journey happened during an exchange in Japan in the last year of my degree, where both architectural and visual ideas chimed. A year before the exchange I struggled with putting my conceptual ideas on paper, but generating ideas outside my comfort zone eventually led to me finding my voice.

FIND ME:

Inspiration

In the first year of my architecture degree, I was desperately trying to figure out a concept for my first design when my wonderful tutor, Brian Adams, said that concept itself has a vague meaning – instead, just think of materials, place, space, light. Take control of the fundamentals, before you dive into concepts and socially impactful ideas. Now, the concept of the drawing and the architectural concept are significantly different matters. In my case, the drawing is a tool, which helps me to communicate my design idea. My advice would be to sketch everything that resonates deeply with you and then analyse every little sketch. It doesn't need to be architecture – it could even be a film scene or a piece of clothing. Why did you notice it? What was so attractive about it? Try to understand your choices. It may give you a little clue, which eventually leads you to finding your style or design concept. You will find your strengths through experiments, which you can endlessly master.

Process

Even though I have a straightforward methodology in place, every time I start a new drawing for a new project, I wonder what it will look like. Methodology comes from testing. Once you find your way and your strength, you can create your method. Studying the work of those who inspire you helps to understand their processes. I followed video tutorials by Mateusz Urbanowicz and his watercolour series of *Tokyo Storefronts*. I brought this knowledge to Hanoi, where I continued to draw facades, but referring to real buildings. Eventually those exercises transferred to my final thesis design and visual style years later. I would always refer to the drawing which inspires me, and keep it on the desk when preparing the final visuals for a crit. Structure in your work also helps – from understanding the process of producing the visualisation to planning the entire final presentation. Sketch it out, prepare the inspiration image, decide on the colour palette and technique. If you are just beginning to understand the graphic design, composition and colours, start from the basics, and work with just black and white and simple views. Let your design talk. Visualisation is just a helping hand for your architecture. Most important – it should be an enjoyable process! Create ☺

ランドリー

Karina Armanda

Tips

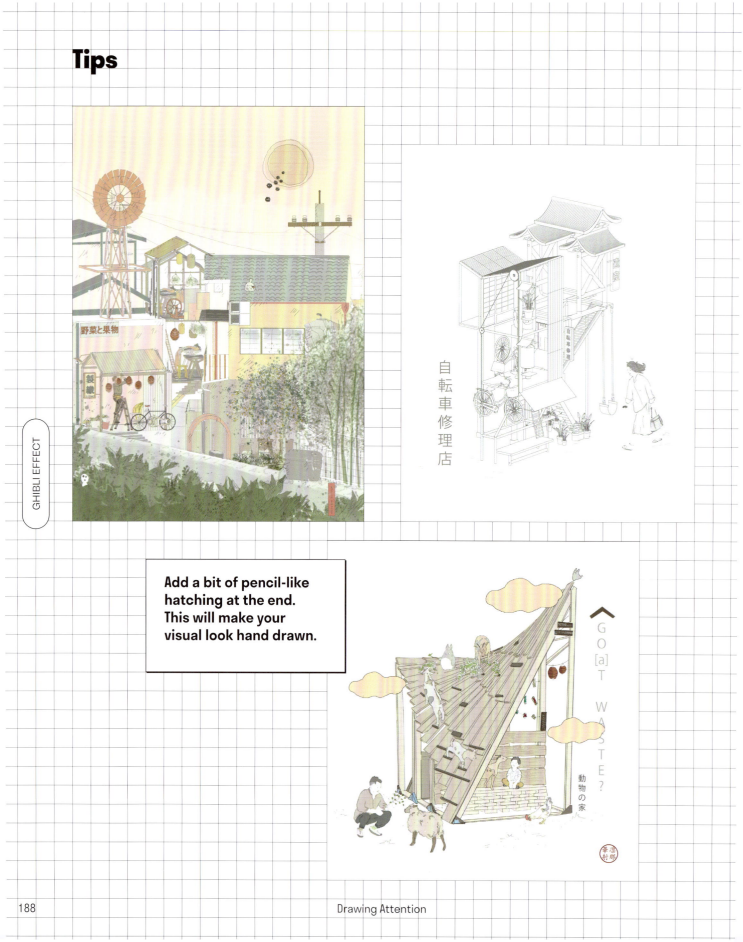

野菜と果物

製麺

自転車修理店

Add a bit of pencil-like
hatching at the end.
This will make your
visual look hand drawn.

GO[a]T WASTE?

動物の家

This design was produced in three hours. Sometimes within the tightest deadlines the best work is delivered.

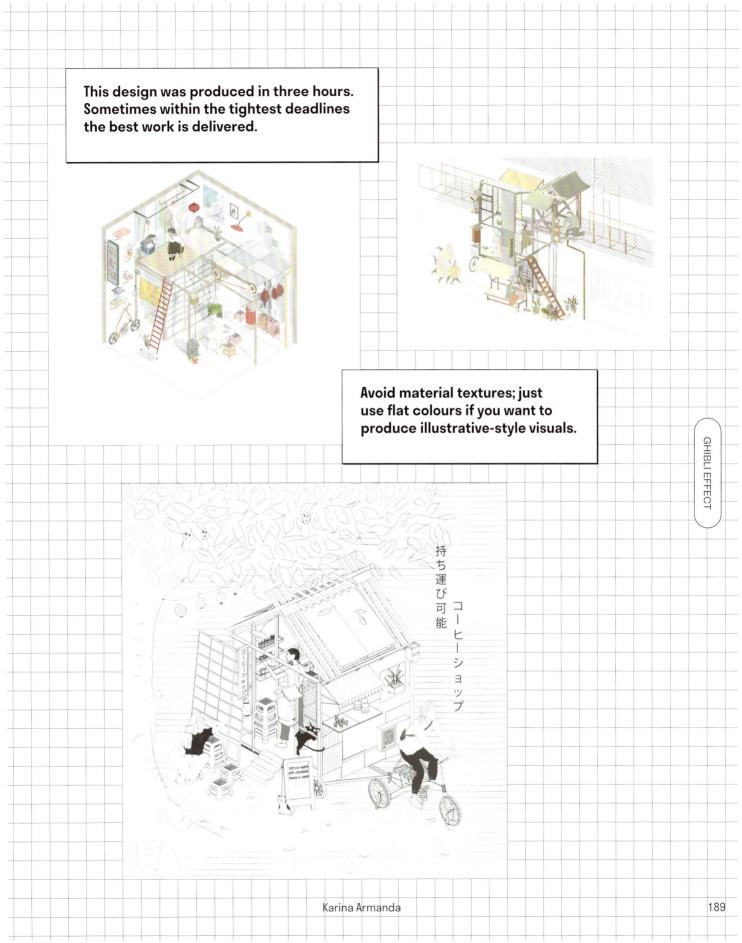

Avoid material textures; just use flat colours if you want to produce illustrative-style visuals.

Karina Armanda

Step by Step

This illustration is described as a bicycle repair station, but it wasn't intentionally designed for a specific function or architectural language. It represents a speculative narrative of participatory build intervention, which is intended to grow organically following the necessity of its users. It is a collection of urban patterns observed in the closest surroundings of the site, which I sketched or took a photograph of; I analysed, arranged, understood, created a narrative. I was inspired by *ukiyo-e* woodblock prints, which eventually influenced the colour palette, texture and certain drawing elements. The thesis idea was dedicated to participatory, self-build, incremental philosophies of architecture. In a similar manner, Japanese woodblock prints represented the collaborative work (*hanmoto* system).

Tools: Adobe Photoshop, SketchUp, AutoCad, Veikk or Wacom drawing pad

GHIBLI EFFECT

1.

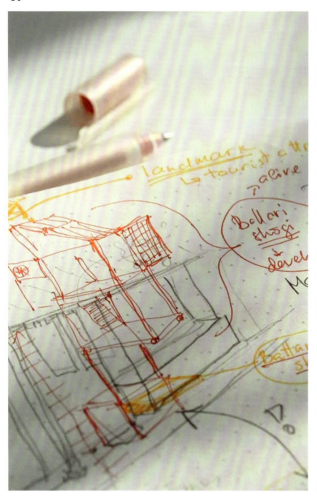

Sketch the idea, mainly to get a grasp of the composition. As you can see, the final model looks more developed. All initial thoughts are in the sketchbook; all the detailed work is in 3D software.

2.

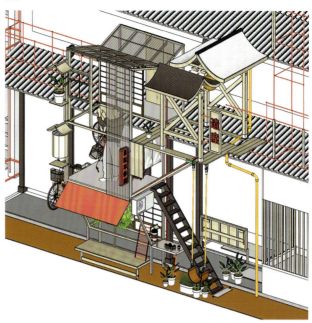

SketchUp is good for 3D modelling. Any components lacking, such as flowerpots, bicycles or downpipes, can be downloaded through 3D Warehouse. **SketchUp** is basic for rather complex modelling, so don't worry if some parts are not as detailed as you desire – you can correct things later in **AutoCAD** or **Photoshop**.

3.

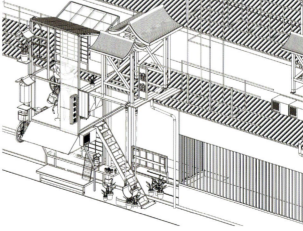

Once you have finalised the model in **SketchUp**, select Parallel view and export the 2D graphics as a DWG file. Save the scene – you will need it later! Now you can correct line weights in **AutoCAD** – set the line weights between 0.05 and 0.09. Now, export the drawing as a PDF.

4.

Jump back to the **SketchUp** scene, and choose 'HiddenLine' style. Untick 'Edges' and 'Profiles' in the 'Edit' section – you should now see shadows without the outline of the building. Alter the 'Shadow' settings to your liking and geolocation. Export in JPEG format.

5.

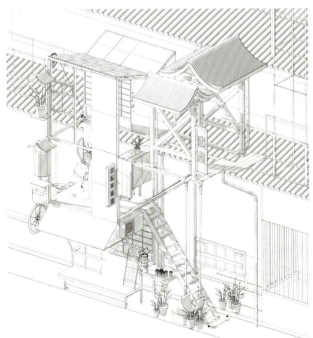

Place the PDF export of the line drawing from **AutoCAD** into **Photoshop**. Place the JPEG export of the shadows and align them.

6.

Choose the colour palette. I suggest choosing a maximum of five colours and using various shades of those colours. You can refer to some existing colour palettes online at the beginning.

7.

Manually select every part of the line drawing using the Magic Wand tool. Create a separate layer for every colour, and add those colours step by step. Consider starting from the structure.

8.

Don't underestimate the importance of filling the drawing with small objects, fun characters, animals and people. You can collage them by finding some online, or trace/draw your own using a drawing pad.

9.

The last step is covering the entire coloured part of the drawing in texture. Here, handmade or watercolour paper textures were used. Change the texture layer settings from 'Normal' to 'Multiple', and also play with opacity – but don't make it too bright ... 10–15% is optimal.

10.

The drawing is ready. Now you can play a little with the saturation or levels (in case the colours are too vivid). If you are using a drawing pad, you can add a little hatching or tiny strokes on the edges of the structure. This will give a hand-drawn, illustrative feel to the drawing.

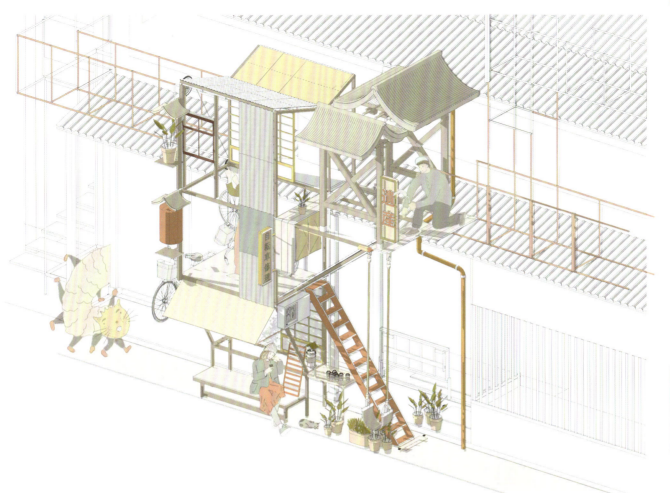

Karina Armanda

"The act of representation is deeply personal as you engage your own reading in it."

Paper Narratives
Pauline Personeni

Title:
Architect, illustrator, editor

Instagram:
@pa.per.narratives

Story

Pictures, writings and books; mediums that are at the edge of the building process fascinate me. Looking at the architectural object from a distance, they have the potential to criticise, complement and influence. I have a collection of both ordinary and happy memories linking my daily life to illustrations, from childhood doodles to recent achievements. But many of these joyful moments are tainted by doubts – *am I able to do it?* – exhaustion – *why so many tedious efforts?* – and frustration – *is it meaningful?* Generating ideas can feel uncomfortable, and the mental struggle you handle when creating and showing your work can be hard. Don't forget that the difficulty of the creative process can help to produce the best work.

Architectural drawing is a way to express more while saying less. Indeed, an illustration is an edited version of a reality, a representation of an object. It is not the object. The illustration does not submit to the strict rules of the object – architecture – but follows its own set of rules – the freedom of creation. The act of representation is deeply personal as you engage your own reading in it: you are the one setting the rules. For each crafted design, I ask myself: can you feel the author in this work?

FIND ME:

Inspiration

Mentors are the real influencers. You never become interested by the work and techniques of an architect or artist by luck, but because someone you trust introduced it to you. It might be a schoolteacher, a work colleague, a social media account, an author. Before focusing on methodology and plain process, mindfully select your mentors. As illustrator, we play the role of mediator: we add or subtract from the project depending on what we wish to narrate. For this reason, some people will argue that drawings can hide reality. It might be true; an illustration can be a form of conscious lie, hiding elements instead of helping us to see beyond. However, we still have the option of doing things with honesty. I've learned to be mindful of my decisions when I set the hierarchy of concepts, as I consider I have both power over and a duty towards the displayed object.

More than a *strong and original* concept, I advocate for a *clear and defined* concept. Should the concept be the only concern of the illustrator? I don't think so. While my work is personal, I cannot simply 'make' an image from scratch. I need an exchange with someone to work for or collaborate with, to get inspired by the story behind the project.

Process

I follow a five-step workflow: inspiration (story and challenges), figuration (3D model and linework), composition (scenario and framing), post-production (life and effects) and communication (export and share). Nevertheless, it is a fluid and organic process. I've tried to develop an eclectic range of techniques which allow me to adapt the illustration to the project (line, render, drawing, collage, realistic, fantastic, classic, unique …).

Before drawing, always ask yourself: for who and what? It is not about the image created but what message needs to be understood through it; this message is coming from the identity of the client, the essence of the project, the purpose of the image, the public to whom it is addressed. It is about non-standardisation: always do the same things but never in the same way, or never do the same things but always in the same way. Both methods will lead you to a unique result.

Tips

Do yourself a favour and make the difference between working hard and working smart. Purchasing *expensive* material is not required. However, purchasing *good* material is an indispensable investment for your work.

PAPER NARRATIVES

Dwelling in Mallorca, *In the corridor*. Design with Barri Studio.

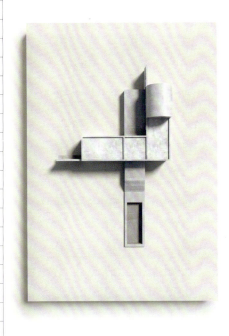

Casa Ter, mock up view. Design by Mesura.

Spot the colour – pay attention to the way colours affect your composition.

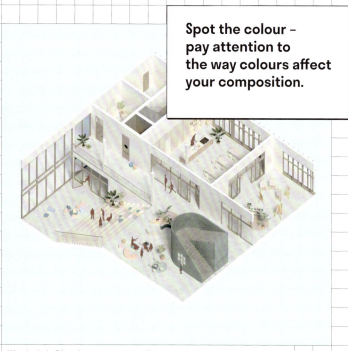

Turn your head upside down to test the quality of your composition. Mirror the image left/right and upside down. See if the balance is conserved.

L'école de la Côte, *Axonometric view*. Design by Microclimat Architecture.

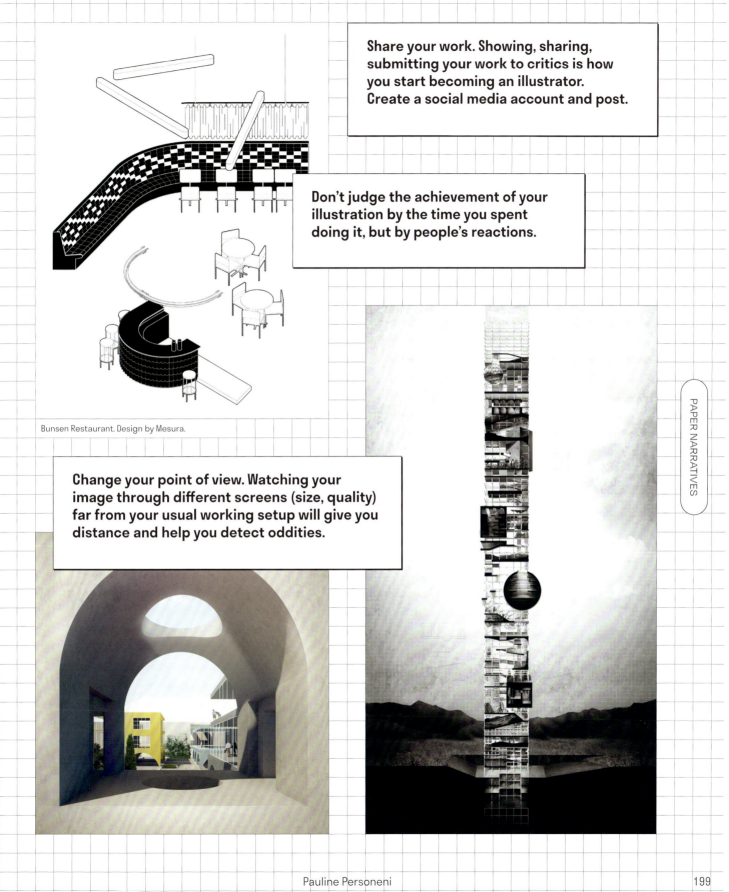

Share your work. Showing, sharing, submitting your work to critics is how you start becoming an illustrator. Create a social media account and post.

Don't judge the achievement of your illustration by the time you spent doing it, but by people's reactions.

Bunsen Restaurant. Design by Mesura.

Change your point of view. Watching your image through different screens (size, quality) far from your usual working setup will give you distance and help you detect oddities.

PAPER NARRATIVES

Step by Step

Inner Talk 4 is part of a series of the same name-gathering personal visual experimentations. They depict architectural artefacts of the palace as a mix of primitive shapes and mysterious gardens, floating among improbable territories. They embody an imaginary vision of our inner worlds, recognisable by their childish colours, vibrant stories and axonometric compositions. The composition displays a palace inhabited by a vivid biotope that blurs our perception of the inside of the building. Balancing between solids and voids, it is letting space for a fantastic landscape to appear within the architecture. While it seems to be floating, the castle is connected to invisible surroundings by stairs. In this case the real interest lies in the process behind the drawing, as the architectural shape is assumed as a pretext for experimentation. Incorporating another of my trademarks, the drawing is built as an axonometric view. It has the double power of showing the truth of a codified orthogonal representation, while offering an uncommon bird's-eye/worm's-eye view on the project. It is a sort of objective basis for a subjective narrative; a world full of potential that mesmerises equally architects and non-architects.

Tools: SketchUp, V-Ray, Photoshop

1.

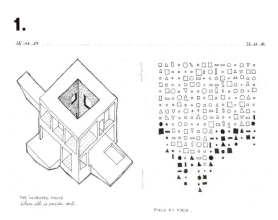

Start with hand-drawn doodles to subconsciously stimulate your creativity. When one of the doodles feels interesting, combine it with a chosen atmosphere and a style according to its aim.

2.

The drawing gives you volumetric and narrative indications; however, the absent colours from the sketch play an essential role in the atmosphere of your composition. A pastel colour palette (beige, pink, green) will mark the calm architectural shape while vivid colour touches provide a cheerful atmosphere.

3.

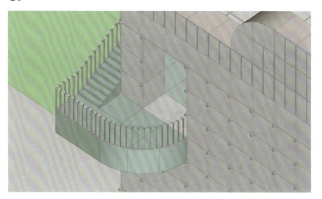

Model the architectural volume based on the preliminary drawing. Get inspired by looking at small details of constructed buildings: doors, handles, handrails, gaps between the walls and the floor, plug sockets, frames, furniture, joints between tiles. Details add depth to your composition.

4.

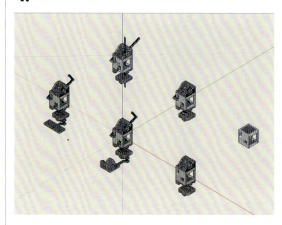

Keep a clean model at all stages by separating the pieces in groups, components and layers. Separating the materials and surfaces by colour will help you easily attribute textures to each element in the next steps.

5.

When the model is set, search for the right way to frame the project. Experiment with points of view in black and white renders to put the emphasis on lighting rather than materials. The final decision depends on the narrative of your project and what element you wish the composition to highlight.

6.

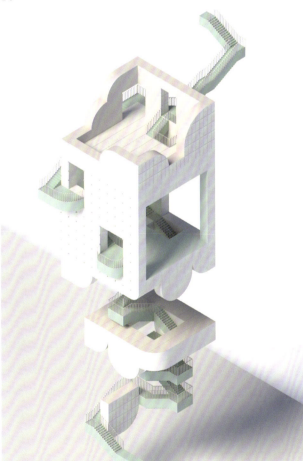

Render – **V-Ray** for **SketchUp** is simple and efficient – and export different layers to be able to add, select and isolate details such as the material, shadows, lights, contrast, normals and texture of the image.

7.

The first image out of the render software may be flat and dull. You can work in 3D to get a subtle result earlier in the process, although it will reduce your freedom during the post-production phase. If the focus is not meant to be on the realistic aspect of the volumes, post-production is a big step in the illustration.

8.

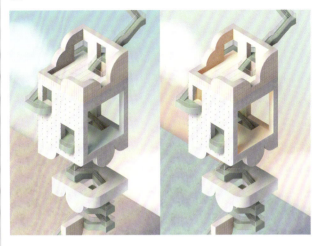

Test different colour settings to play with the hierarchy of the elements in the composition. For example, add yellow touches to give the impression of glow on the main focal point, or adapt the colour of an element that isn't satisfying. Adjust colour, change contrast and adapt throughout the process.

9.

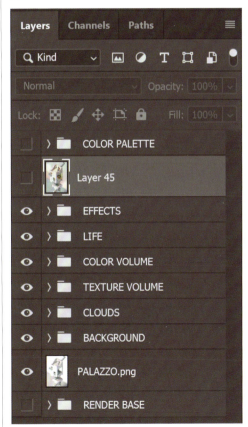

Keep your layers and groups neatly labelled. The structure needs to be intuitive and simple; the more complex your composition, the more thankful you will be to have an optimised file.

10.

Use mixed techniques to make the drawing unique: a rendered view will contrast with collages and enhance a paradox between realistic elements (shadows, materiality) versus fantastic ones (colours, life). Carefully select and cut out the shapes you need, as the quality of your final export will depend on them.

11.

Add signs of life such as botanical details through collage elements. Search for images that are free to use, with a vintage botanical illustration twist. The plants are mainly green with touches of intense coral. All the biotope parts are inside the volume and grow from it with vivid colours that contrast with the architecture.

12.

When the image is complete, export it in several formats: low resolution (72 dpi) to high (300 dpi), in CMYK to print or RGB to share online. That way you will have ready any type of file you could need to display your work. Last but not least, share the result: publish it online, print it, offer it to a friend, but let go of it.

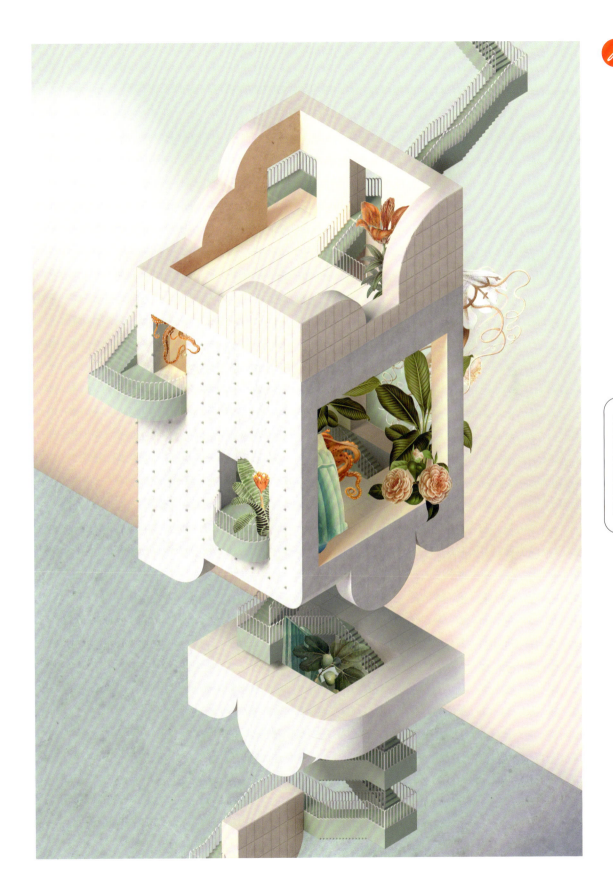

Pauline Personeni

"I draw to discover myself and my architecture."

Art of Entropy
Neil Spiller

Title:
Architect, professor of architecture, editor of *Architectural Design* (formerly), Hawksmoor Chair of Architecture and Landscape, University of Greenwich, Vice Dean and Graduate Director of Design, Bartlett UCL

Instagram:
@neilspiller0

Story

In the early 1980s, I became interested in and inspired by visionary architectural drawings – particularly by Cedric Price, Archigram and Lebbeus Woods – and began to experiment with architectural graphics as a student. What drives some architects to make drawings and models of architectures that are clientless and therefore unbuilt or currently unbuildable? What is architecture, and can it be held within a drawing/model as well as a building?

Architecture is a synthesis of poetry, fine art and sculpture; it flows over time like music and its spaces have establishing vignettes; it oscillates across the scales (from macro to micro) with denouement like film or prose. Above all, architecture is the manipulation of space in all its manifestations. Space can be imagined, and space can be graphically represented.

FIND ME:

Inspiration

During 2000, my monograph *Maverick Deviations* was published as a 'greatest hits album' of ten or so projects drawn from 1985 to 1998, lovingly graphically designed by Vaughan Oliver and V23. It was a cathartic moment. I knew from then on, I wanted to create a long project that took years to develop and push the envelope of what might constitute architecture and architectural drawing in the 21st century. No more the blunting form and prose in the hope of getting a commission. It was time to admit, once and for all, what I am: an experimental architect adept at creating, strange, meaningful worlds.

At first, the ideas for this project were ill-defined. Like much of my previous work, I knew it must explore the impact of advanced technology on architectural design. Swiftly, a universe of things and spaces that changed their sensitivity in sympathy with many disparate inputs emerged, dancing to a song of love and talking to each other in simultaneously diverse languages. The project blossomed into a vast undertaking of hundreds of drawings and it resided, mostly, on a psycho-geographical island, half-existing and half-imagination. This is the macro concept within which all my work since 1998 has evolved and is now known as the 'Communicating Vessels' project.

Process

Love, life and drawings; so individual, human and imperative. Drawing helps to describe the world and our perception of it. To each of us, the world is different and constantly being redrafted. My work involves drawn architectural speculations that investigate virtuality, biotechnology, nanotechnology, augmented and mixed realities and reflexive architectures. The drawing is not a passive, one-way architectural occupation, but a symbiotic relationship where the drawer can learn from the drawing and the act of making a drawing can inform the overall concept, idea and scope of architecture by the act of rereading, post-rationalisation and chance. The drawing informs my writing, and vice-versa.

This is often intuitive initially; the drawings are ongoing design conversations. In a cybernetic way, the author designs their work by intellectually building it through constructing the drawing. There is a dialogue between the drawer and the drawing that is constantly changing its syntax, lexicon and attenuation. This method gives a wide horizon of possible compositional, but more importantly conceptual, outcomes. The drawing is a laboratory for researching architectural space and objects. I use multiple techniques and media to produce work; anything is fair game.

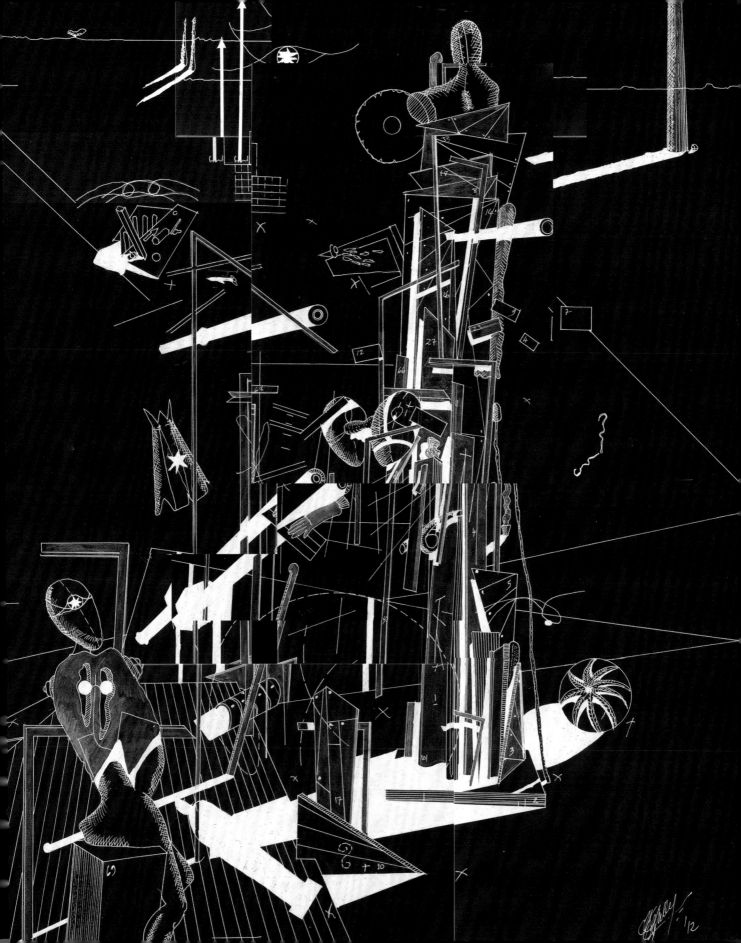

Tips

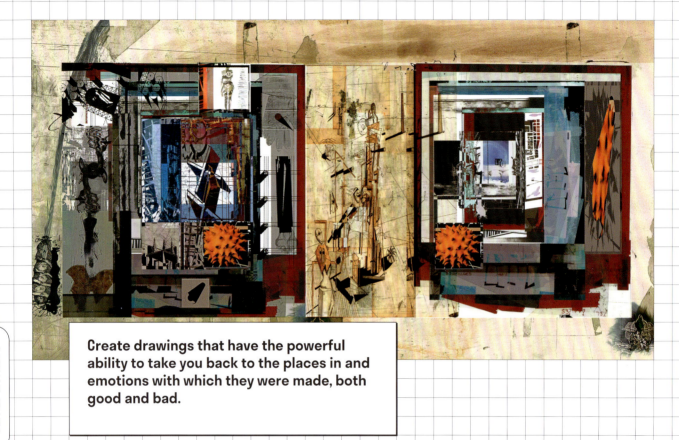

Create drawings that have the powerful ability to take you back to the places in and emotions with which they were made, both good and bad.

Do not be afraid of post-rationalising a drawing and letting it take you on an un-preconceived architectural journey.

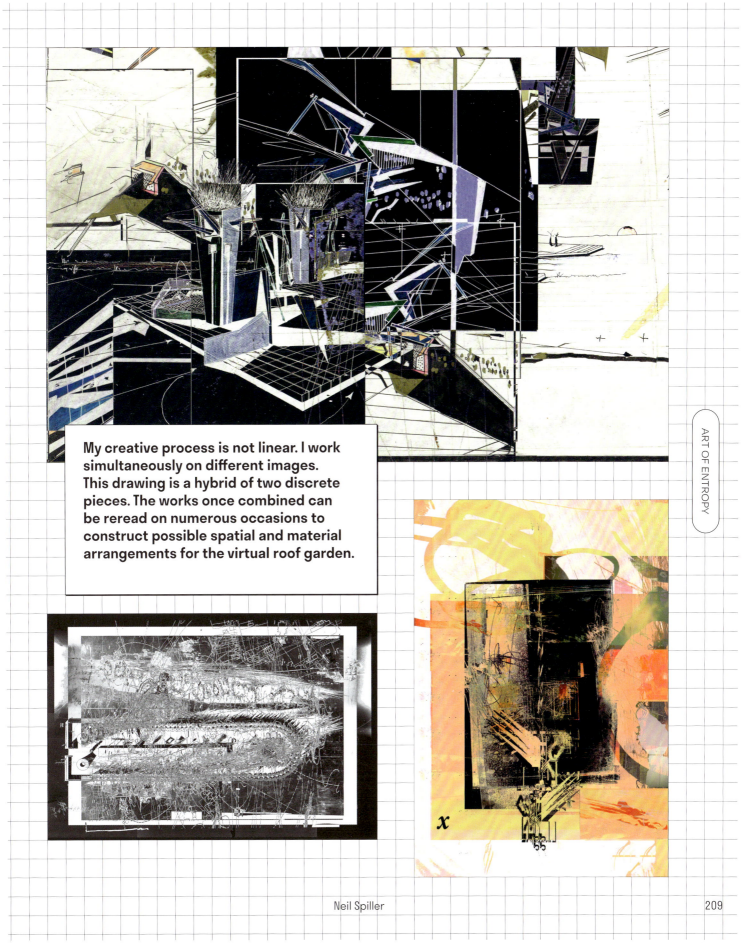

My creative process is not linear. I work simultaneously on different images. This drawing is a hybrid of two discrete pieces. The works once combined can be reread on numerous occasions to construct possible spatial and material arrangements for the virtual roof garden.

Step by Step

The 'Communicating Vessels' project is a memory theatre folding the history of art and literature in on itself, and often memorialises important, inspirational people that I have become friends with – one being Lebbeus Woods (*The Walled Garden for Lebbeus*), another being a set of drawings for the augmented reality roof garden for Vaughan Oliver, who sadly died at the end of 2019 after our friendship of 30 years. Vaughan Oliver was one of the most respected graphic designers and art directors in the world. Many graphic designers quote him as a heroic inspiration for them.

> The rusted implements of underground torture. The sleeping sirens floating in shallows. The aliens made purely of distended eyeballs. The loveless beds, gelatinous hearts, topless flamenco dancers and monkeys cowering amid sinister numerical runes.
>
> Mark Beaumont in 'RIP Vaughan Oliver', *New Musical Express*[7]

The 'Communicating Vessels' project is a self-instigated drawn and written theoretical architectural design project. The project was initiated in 1998 and finished with the Longhouse. The bulk of the project is positioned on an island in Britain's smallest town, Fordwich, just outside Canterbury in Kent. Rather than a traditional architectural site, it is a psycho-geographical site that holds memories of childhood for the author.

Technology is allowing architects to mix and augment real objects with virtual ones; to question the inertness of materials and, vicariously, architecture; to link and network electronically all manner of spaces and scales of phenomena together; to create reflexive spatial relationships. These drawings are an augmented reality roof garden in honour of Vaughan that is much larger than the actual roof of the Longhouse.

This recent work includes a set of drawings that were not preconceived and led to all sorts of places in an attempt to confront the blank sheet, dislocate the architectural self and push my architecture into uncharted waters.

ART OF ENTROPY

1.

Content Aware Plan, 2020
Erasure and chance is part of my creative process. **Photoshop** has a feature called 'Content Aware', which allows the computer to decide what to replace a highlighted area with, by sampling the content of what's left and inserting something else from what it has gleaned. This drawing was made by repeating this instruction.

2.

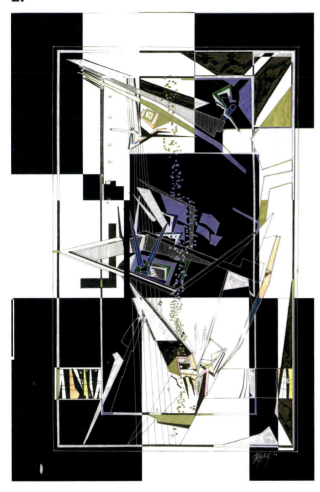

Initial Drawing, 2020 – possible plan forms
This drawing was constructed fully by hand on A1 white mounting board, using a 0.5 Rotring ink pen, Japanese coloured pencils and a gold felt-tip pen. It was then scanned in sections with an A4 scanner, tiled together and some tiles inverted in **Photoshop**.

3.

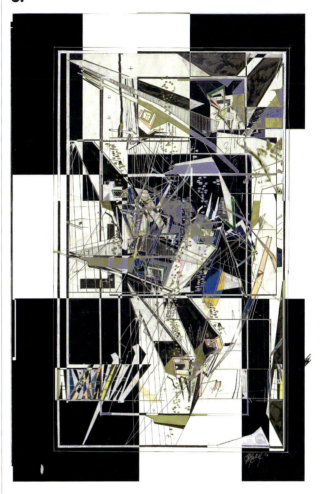

Composite Plan, 2020
A series of plans were developed to try to define a choreography of the virtual dance of these towers over time. This was done in **Photoshop**, compositing images together, manipulating and multiplying them, then creating further images to provoke possible articulations.

4. [Overleaf]

Perspective View, 2020
This second drawing is an attempt to explore the topology of the roof garden and a series of memorial towers containing some of Vaughan Oliver's famous motifs (the haloed monkey and the broken knife, for example). Hand drawing as above and then scanned, partially inverted then overlaid in **Photoshop** on scan of a piece of my drawing board.

Capturing Culture
Areesha Khalid

Title:
**RIBA Part II MArch student,
freelance illustrator**

Instagram:
@architecturebyari

Remember how you felt walking down that narrow inner-city street, bustling with life? Catching snippets of conversations in the native language among passing people, all dressed in the unique styles of the land. The surrounding shopfronts vividly lit and the scent of street food luring you in as you embrace all the culture this street has to offer.

Now, how do you express this vibrant culture that all five of your senses experienced in one still image?

The spaces that we occupy tend to soak in the culture of people they house. The built environment can tell stories through colour, pattern, signage, and wear and tear. Capturing this 'lived in' quality of space is essentially what conveys culture.

It's the people that make the culture, so your first point of contact should be locals. If applicable, this could even be you. Talk to locals about their favourite spot in the city, a fond memory of their childhood home or something relevant to your research. Often this memory will be embedded in a space which they are able to vividly recall, expressing minute atmospheric details that hold sentimental or cultural value and therefore have stuck with them. This could be the peace of shade provided by thick vines wrapping their balcony, the sound of splashing water in their courtyard fountain during the peak of summer, or the earthy scent of rain touching the dry soil, signalling monsoon. Take note of these details; they will convey the essence of culture and longing in your drawing.

Next, visualise your narrative. Begin to recreate this image, a collaboration between the local's verbal account and your creative spatial reconstruction informed by an understanding of the culture. Start by collecting imagery of specific elements that were mentioned through historical records, fashion campaigns and media. Once you have enough supporting material you can begin drawing.

Start with a specific element such as an intricate vernacular tile pattern or outfit that stood out, and draw the rest of the scene around it. For instance, if starting with a street food item, form a narrative around this; how is this usually sold? What does the typography of the stall look like? Who is selling this? And what is the embedded cultural significance of this food – is it rainy-evening or hot-summer-day food? Answer these questions through drawing to enrich its cultural quality.

Following your narrative, sketch out the base drawing with a pen/line tool, adhering to standard architectural line weight rules. Adding maximum details at this stage will give a sense of identity to the image whereby at a glance, one can place it in the precise cultural context; traditional facade displays and motifs, native-language street signs, clothing designs, wall posters, etc. It's all in the details! Follow up with colour from a well-researched, curated palette; colours have specific cultural connotations indigenous to particular regions, so you can use this as a tool. When colouring, start with the largest background objects, eventually moving down to smaller foreground details; this will help you achieve overall tonal harmony.

The final, game-changing step to push the atmospheric value and induce a sensory viewer experience is to introduce light and weather. Using a blur colour tool, add locally used light sources such as lanterns, candles, string lights for night views or soft, directional sun rays for daytime. Focus light around any element you wish to draw attention to.

Lastly, take a step back and see if the final image still conveys the original ideas. If you still have access to the locals you spoke with, test to see if your drawing evokes nostalgia for them.

Remember how you felt walking down that narrow inner-city street, taking in all the culture with your five senses? You now have a drawing that can convey similar warmth through a still image.

Drawing on The Future

Hamza Shaikh

As the next generation of architecture students and young professionals emerge, so too will new cultures, practices and institutions. The graduates of the early 2000s are becoming the directors and CEOs of today, bringing with them a greater acceptance of change and innovation. The field of architecture, particularly in the UK, continues to deliver outstanding individuals and companies, creating spaces, buildings and cities to the highest level. However, our profession is not an easy one – and this is particularly true for graduates, who must bear the burden of poor pay and slow career progression in the most inflated of economic times. Perhaps this is why, increasingly, we are seeing a movement of architecturally trained professionals venturing further than traditional architectural practice, where pay is often better, and their vastly wide-ranging creative skills can be utilised. They are architects turned tech-entrepreneurs; acclaimed ateliers; material engineers; user-experience specialists; set designers; writers and historians; and filmmakers. Despite some of the failures of architectural education in preparing students for practice, the potential it offers for wider contribution is immense.

Education and practice, especially in the UK, are going through enormous change. A survey carried out by the Architects Registration Board recently concluded that major changes would take place transforming the educational route to professional qualification – the most significant changes in the last half-century.[8] The Building Safety Act 2022 has already initiated major reforms in the building industry due to the Grenfell tragedy. These changes have begun to put architects in completely new territory, with new roles and responsibilities. Furthermore, the next generation of architects are emerging with vehemently different ethical and cultural outlooks. Disruptive technological innovations such as virtual reality, artificial intelligence and rapidly evolving parametric tools are now beginning to establish themselves in architectural workflows and services. We are in a moment of great flux.

All these signs point to massive transformations in our field, and within five years, I believe, the 'architect' will be perceived by society very differently. That new perception and our new roles will be determined by us. This book may seem to point towards the role of the 'architect as artist' being revived; however, my personal outlook is one that encourages greater flexibility and variation of services in practice. In fact some practices have already begun doing this, facilitated by the diverse skillsets architecture graduates attain from university education. Architecture students of the future will likely gain even wider experience in architecture school with flexible learning paths – some favouring traditional professional roles within the built industry and others encouraging graduates to flourish entrepreneurially. Ultimately, the major issues our field faces represent an opportunity for reset.

However, as we continue to question our roles as architects in a fast-changing world and question the future of our profession, we mustn't forsake our rich historical foundations. Recognising the efforts of our predecessors and heeding their works gives us a powerful footing from which to contribute to the historical discourse – hence this book begins with a historical framing. For those who are influencing progression in our field, they do so while standing on the shoulders of giants. My personal journey in writing this book has been humbling, as I found revelatory answers and work from those who came before us.

My aim throughout this book and its underlying concept has been to express the fundamental need for architects to communicate their boundless value through the universal passion and skill of artistic expression. I hope to have shown that our value as architectural practitioners exceeds the sole outcome of manifesting a building. Our core skillsets of visionary thinking, narrativisation, and systematic problem-solving show that our scope for contribution to society is far greater than what we do currently. By going one layer deeper, we discover that the root of communicating these values is inherent in achieving greater prosperity.

It is no coincidence that millions of practitioners and students across the world are flocking to social media and being inspired by architectural illustrators, influencers and practitioners pushing the boundaries. These are individuals, collectives and practices who are breaking the mould, unbound by the chains of gatekeeping forces – free to express their truths and build their brands. You will have known or learned by now that one such niche that truly dominates in this revolution is 'architectural drawings on social media', and Instagram more specifically. Why, might you ask? The ability to translate ideas, thoughts and dreams into artistic expressions so that they may forever exist in a tangible albeit digital form of reality is the survival skill we need in a cut-throat industry. It's what makes us unique and increases the value of our offering. Drawing attention, or more specifically, communicating artistic expression, is our greatest asset as architcotural practitioners, and we must never lose this.

About the Contributors

Ehab Alhariri is a Syrian American architect and digital artist based in Dubai, UAE. He studied architecture at Damascus University. After graduating in 2007, he gained a lot of experience from working as an architectural designer between Dubai and Washington DC. His designs have been featured in Architizer and CNN Arabic, among other news outlets.

Ana Aragão graduated as an architect from the Faculty of Architecture of the University of Porto. Her projects include participation in the Italian Pavilion (Venice Biennale 2021), and she was selected by Lürzer's Archive as one of the 200 Best Illustrators Worldwide (2014). Her last exhibition was 'No plan for Japan' (Orient Museum, Lisbon 2021–2022), with works also appearing in Lisbon's MAAT (2022).

Karina Armanda graduated from the Glasgow School of Art and completed her graduation project in Kyoto, Japan researching participatory and DIY methods in architecture. Karina is currently exploring how through small architectural interventions and workshops she can address the environmental crisis and engage local communities.

Bryan Cantley has worked in the Permanent Collection at SFMOMA and has lectured and exhibited internationally. He is a recipient of a Graham Grant. His monograph *Mechudzu* was published in 2011, and the follow-up, *Speculative Coolness*, will be published in 2023.

David Drazil is an architect who loves to sketch. He's the founder of SketchLikeAnArchitect.com, an author of three books on architectural sketching, a content creator and an online teacher with more than 12,000 students on his courses.

Yvette Earl is a freelance illustrator based in the North of England. When she's not drawing or designing you'll find her snapping lots of photographs, painting or walking.

Hammad Haider is an architectural assistant, urban sketcher, freelance illustrator and Arabic calligrapher based in Yorkshire, currently completing his MA at the University of Sheffield. With a passion for travel and hand drawing, Hammad's work embodies a rich cultural narrative tied in with raw architectural representation.

Veronika Ikonnikova is an architect and illustrator based in Tokyo. Originally from Ukraine, she came to Japan following a deep interest in Japanese aesthetics and design. After graduating from the University of Tokyo, she has been working as an architect in Tokyo, while pursuing art and illustration alongside an architectural career.

Areesha Khalid is currently studying for her MArch (RIBA Part II) at Westminster. Areesha depicts her rich cultural heritage and South Asian roots through spatial imagery that evokes a sense of nostalgia for viewers. She runs an Instagram page and print shop, @ architecturebyari, sharing drawings with the South Asian diaspora across the globe.

Saul Kim is an architectural designer based in Seoul. He holds a bachelor's degree in architecture from Southern California Institute of Architecture and a Master's degree in architecture from Harvard Graduate School of Design. He is also an instructor at Domestika, a global online learning platform with 8 million users.

Perry Kulper is an architect and an associate professor of architecture at the University of Michigan's Taubman College of Architecture and Urban Planning.

Clement Luk Laurencio (@clementluklaurencio) is an architectural designer and artist, and was the Invited Juror for the DOTY 2021 competition. He currently lectures about his drawing practice, Drawing (Spatial) Fictions. He completed his BArch (RIBA Part I) at the University of Nottingham, and MArch (RIBA Part II) at the Bartlett School of Architecture, UCL.

Malavika Madhuraj is a designer in Studio Gang, New York. She has always understood design as the core in finding new and creative solutions for tackling practical issues and believes in a multidisciplinary approach. She holds a Master of Science in Advanced Architectural Design from Columbia University GSAPP and a Bachelor of Architecture from VIT University, India.

Bea Martin is a senior lecturer in Architecture/Architecture Technology at the University of Huddersfield, where she is also the BA (Hons) Architecture programme director. She is the owner of Speculative Assemblies, an experimental design lab exploring the visual construct in architecture. Her research explores the critical uses of drawing in architectural design thinking and introduces the idea of operative drawing as a methodological process.

Salmaan Mohamed is a freelance architectural designer and illustrator from Chennai, India. He trusts drawing as a creative and necessary tool to develop his designs, both analogue and digital. He has created architectural drawings for his personal projects as well as other international architectural retail and spatial design firms.

Fraser Morrison is an architect, teacher and researcher who incorporates innovative technologies and circularity principles in his work. Having featured in exhibitions and journals, he combines machine learning with traditional drafting techniques to design, illustrate, explore and implement low-carbon architecture.

Pauline Personeni has worked as an architect, editor, and communication consultant. Having graduated with a Master's degree in architecture, she now focuses her work on establishing communication between architecture and the public. The tools she uses to shape communication strategies range from illustration to theoretical approaches, as well as book editing.

Thomas Rowntree is an MArch student and content creator. His brand is tomrowstudios, which showcases the behind-the-scenes and life of a practising architect through vlogs on YouTube and short-form content on Instagram.

Hamza Shaikh is a London-based architectural designer. He is also a prominent architectural illustrator on social media where he shares his popular experimental drawings with a large and growing following. He is the host of the Two Worlds Design podcast series which aims to uncover the hidden potential of architecture by speaking with extraordinary practitioners. In 2021, he was the recipient of the Individual of the Year award by the Thornton Education Trust for 'inspiring future generations' in architecture. Hamza has been described as a rising star and an influencer in the profession and is seen as a mentor to young professionals and students. He is also a regular visiting critic at the University for the Creative Arts and the University of Westminster.

Neil Spiller is editor of *AD*, and previously he was Hawksmoor Chair of Architecture and Landscape and Deputy Pro Vice-Chancellor of the University of Greenwich, London. Before this he was Vice-Dean and Graduate Director of Design at the Bartlett School of Architecture, UCL. He is an internationally renowned visionary architect.

s.y.h is a practising architect and illustrator based in London. s.y.h creates intricate isometric illustrations drawing inspiration from architecture, film and art.

Sana Tabassum is a social entrepreneur, content creator and MArch student at the University of Greenwich. She founded :scale (to-scale), an architecture blog and platform for students and young designers, in order to create an inclusive and collaborative archi-community that champions a balance between wellbeing and productivity.

Zain Al-Sharaf Wahbeh (@designs.by.zain) is a London-based Palestinian researcher and designer, born in Jordan and raised in the United Arab Emirates. She obtained her Part I qualification in architecture from the University of Edinburgh in 2019 and her Part II qualification from the Royal College of Art in 2022.

Eric Wong is a practising architect and an architecture design tutor who has taught at undergraduate and postgraduate level. He has also worked on animated feature films as a concept artist and production designer. His architectural journey has been influenced by critical thinking, speculative architecture and intricate line drawings.

Endnotes

1   J Kauffman, *Drawing on Architecture: The Object of Lines, 1970–1990*, Cambridge, MA, The MIT Press, 2018.

2   Ibid.

3   Ibid.

4   L Woods, *Radical Reconstruction*, New York, Princeton Architectural Press, 1997. This interpretation of the drawings, words and ideas of Lebbeus Woods explores issues that deal with the design of systems in crisis, where the order of the existing is being confronted by the order of the new. Wood's designs are politically charged and provocative visions of a possible reality.

5   Adapted from G Deleuze and F Guattari, *On the Line*, New York, Columbia University, Semiotext(e), 1983.

6   *Rooftop Urbanism: Usage and Potential of Rooftop Space in the Urban Environment*, Re-search Project, 2018. More information can also be found at rooftopurbanism.com.

7   Mark Beaumont, 'RIP Vaughan Oliver: The visionary 4AD artist who defined the aesthetic of a subculture', *New Musical Express*, https://www.nme.com/features/vaughan-oliver-pixies-artist-4ad-obituary-2591970, 2 January 2020.

8   Architects Registration Board, 'ARB announces fundamental reforms to architectural education', Architects Registration Board, https://arb.org.uk/arb-announces-fundamental-reforms-to-architectural-education-2/, 7 October 2021.